The Greville Estate:
the history of a Kilburn neighbourh(

Marianne Colloms *&* Dick Weindling

Opposite   The Greville Estate in 1868 (estate boundary
shown as white dotted line)

Cover   Kilburn tollgate on Maida Vale (see p 16)

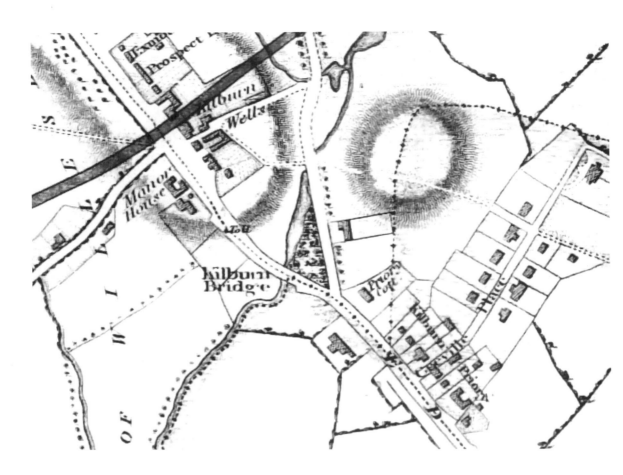

The Greville Estate, 1845. The route of the London to Birmingham railway is shown by the thick dark line above Kilburn Wells. There was no station at Kilburn until 1852. The Kilbourne stream runs south under the railway to cross Edgware Road at Kilburn Bridge. Development on the estate is confined to the houses of Kilburn Priory on Edgware Road, the properties facing the unnamed private road, and the villas of Greville Place. A footpath from St John's Wood crosses Greville Place and the Hilly Field, en route to Kilburn Wells. The hill is shown by the hatched circle, bisected by the boundary between Hampstead and St Marylebone parishes

The Greville Estate:

the history of a Kilburn neighbourhood

Marianne Colloms & Dick Weindling

Occasional paper no.6
Camden History Society, 2007

ISBN 978-0-904491-68-5

Acknowledgements

Thanks are due to the following:

Camden Local Studies and Archives Centre staff

Jane Anderson, archivist at Blair Castle,
for information on the Duke of Atholl

John Lewis Partnership Archive Collection,
for permission to reproduce John Spedan Lewis photograph

Raymond Martin, Customer Services, BT Archives

Richard Baldwin, Camden and Islington Cemeteries Service

City of Westminster Archives Centre staff

Contents

List of maps and illustrations

Maps

Illustrations

1 Historical introduction

Kilburn Priory

The earliest history of Kilburn concerns the Priory, a small group of religious buildings dating from the 12th century, near today's Belsize Road. Kilburn Priory appears to have begun when a hermit named Godwyn built a small hermitage at 'Cuneburn' beside a stream. It passed into the ownership of the Abbot of Westminster, who with the agreement of the Bishop of London established a small group of nuns at Kilburn in about 1130. The first three nuns, Emma, Gunhilda and Christina, were formerly maids of honour to Queen Matilda, wife of Henry I. The nuns converted the hermitage into a convent of the Benedictine Order, and Godwyn was appointed chaplain and warden for life.

When Godwyn died a dispute arose about the jurisdiction of the convent between the Bishop of London and the Abbot of Westminster, probably because of the unusual, though not unique, situation of a priory of nuns being dependent on an abbey of monks. The dispute was resolved in favour of the Abbot on the grounds that the 'Cell of Keleburn' had belonged to Westminster since its foundation. In 1225 the Pope issued a Papal Bull confirming that the monks of Westminster Abbey had jurisdiction over the 'Cell of Kyleburn'. But the dispute rumbled on and was only finally settled in 1231, when a compromise was reached between the two sides.

The church erected in connection with the Priory was dedicated to St John the Baptist. Further property was added to the Priory from time to time by different Abbots and benefactors, in return for prayers said for the souls of brethren from Westminster. Soon after the church was dedicated, Abbot Herbert gave the nuns an estate called Gara, in the Manor of Knightsbridge, probably Kensington Gore. The priory also owned land in Surrey, Kent, Buckinghamshire, Tottenham, Southwark and Hendon. The manor farm of Wembley, in the parish of Harrow, also seems to have belonged to Kilburn Priory and the church at Cudham in Kent, was appropriated to Kilburn Priory by the Bishop of Rochester in 1376. Other bequests were made in the form of a 'corrody', a gift of wine and food. Despite these and other additions of land, the Priory never became wealthy and at various times it was exempted from taxes.

An enquiry in 1377 showed Kilburn to be in financial difficulties. The reason being that the Priory was near the Edgware Road, a much-used highway between London and St Albans, and the nuns were obliged to give a free night's lodging to anyone travelling the road. Travellers tended to congregate at the Priory before ascending Shoot-up Hill, waiting to form groups for protection against robbers operating in the dense oak forest farther along the road. At one point the nuns were drawing a weekly allowance of 40 gallons of beer and 28 loaves of bread to sustain these travellers as well as themselves. In 12 weeks in 1500, the nunnery spent 111 shillings on food and drink: meat 49s, fish 24s, ale 12s, beer 17s, wine and spices 4s, bread 2/6, and salt 4s. Other food was probably grown locally. Another 44s was spent on the wages of harvestmen and repairs of farm equipment. Servants' wages amounted to 46s for farm workers, carter, ploughmen, barleymen, and threshers.

The Priory was always a small establishment, with a prioress and four to six nuns. The nuns, often daughters of wealthy men in the City, brought a dowry with them. Occasionally, one absconded: in 1352 a warrant was issued to arrest

Margery Pigeon, a nun of Kilburn, who had run away and was living as a vagabond in secular dress. The names of some of the prioresses can be found in various documents over the years. The earliest known was Alice in 1207-8. A Margery or Margaret is mentioned in 1243-48, to be followed by Joan (1248 to about 1257). Others were Maud (1269), Cecily (1290), Alice de Pommesbourne (1339), Agnes (1345) and Emma de Sancto Omero also known as Emma de St Omer (1397 and 1403), and the last was Anne Browne (1536).

A few tenants on the surrounding farmland can also be identified. Prioress Anne Browne granted a 40-year lease to William Wylde, dated 30 June 1535, for the 18-acre farm called 'The West End', held by William Hille. The valuation of the Priory and estates from *Valor Ecclesiasticus* (*The King's Book*, 1535), lists Wm. Wylde for property in Kylborne Street and West End. In spite of its difficulties the priory continued its daily support for travellers for 400 years until 1536, when it was dissolved as a lesser monastery (value less than £200) by Henry VIII. The 'Nonnerie of Kilnborne' was then valued at only £74 7s 11d, including the Priory, farm outbuildings and 46 acres of land. (Other authorities give values of £86 or £121.)

The best description we have of the priory is an inventory of 11 May 1536 at the dissolution, signed by Anne Browne, which gives details of the rooms and furniture for the church, house, brewhouse and bakehouse. The buildings are described as follows:

1. The Hall, probably the refectory or dinning room.
2. The Chamber next to the Church, which was the nuns' sitting room.
3. The Middle Chamber between that and the Prioress's chamber
   (the nuns' bedroom).
4. The Prioress's Chamber.
5. The Buttery, Pantry and Cellar.
6. The Inner Chamber to the Prioress's Chamber.
7. The Chamber between the Prioress's Chamber and the Hall.
8. The Kitchen.
9. The Larder House.
10. The Brewhouse and Bakehouse.
11. The three Chambers for the Chaplain, and the Hinds or Husbandmen.
12. The Confessor's Chamber.
13. The Church.

The Priory also possessed 'one horse of the collar of blacke', valued at 5s. When the State took control of the Priory, Anne Browne was given a pension of £10 a year.

After the dissolution

The history of ownership of the Priory land after the dissolution is complex. Henry VIII soon exchanged the property with the Order of the Knights of St John of Jerusalem for their manor in Paris Garden, Southwark, which was much more valuable. Four years later, when the larger monasteries were dissolved, Kilburn, still owned by the Order of St John, reverted to the Crown, and was granted to Robert Ratcliffe, Earl of Sussex. In 1546, Edward VI granted it to John Dudley, Earl of Warwick, who immediately sold it to Richard Taverner. He conveyed it to John Lambe in 1550 whose son Richard died 20 January 1567. Richard's daughter Mary Lambe married Edward Josselyn and the estate passed to Henry Josselyn in 1584. He sold it the same year to Sir Henry Gate and his wife. In 1590 Gate's son Edward conveyed it to Sir Arthur Atye.

Sir Arthur died on 2 December 1604, probably at Kilburn Priory, and was buried at Harrow on the Hill. The property passed to his son Robert Atye, who married Jane, the daughter of Sir John St John of Lydiard Tregoze. As they had no male children, the property passed to their daughter Eleanor, who married Sir William Roberts of Willesden. In 1663 Dame Eleanor Roberts and her daughters sold it to Edward Nelthrope, a London merchant, whose daughter married Robert Liddell, grandson of Sir Thomas Liddell, of Ravensworth Castle, County Durham. They had a son, Henry Liddell (d.1768) who devised the estate to his nephew Richard Middleton of Chirk Castle, Denbighshire. In 1773 Middleton divided the property, selling the Shuttup (Shoot Up) Hill estate, together with 40 acres at Kilburn to John Powell of Fulham. The rest of the land at Kilburn, called Abbey Farm, was conveyed to Richard Marsh of Kilburn Bridge. By 1775 the 46 acres of Abbey Farm, on the site of Kilburn Priory, was the property of his son, also called Richard Marsh, of Simonshyde near Hatfield. Then in 1819 his widow Ann Marsh sold the property to Fulk Greville Howard.

Writing in 1814, the Hampstead historian J J Park notes that the remains of the Priory had long since been destroyed, but the site was still distinguishable by a rising bank in a field adjoining Kilburn Wells. The engraving [1] reproduced in Park's *History of Hampstead* shows only one remaining building.

Relics of Kilburn Priory – some pottery, a few coins and a bronze vessel, all medieval – were found in excavations on the Priory site in the autumn of 1852 and were shown at the Archaeological Institute by the builder George Duncan (see chapter 2), but their present whereabouts is unknown. The only other remaining

[1] Sole remains of Kilburn Priory in 1750 (engraving of 1772)

relic of the Priory is a small brass tablet, found in 1877, showing the image of a nun's face **[2]**. This is thought to be that of Emma de St Omer (about 1400), and was probably a portion of a larger brass covering the prioress's tomb. It was placed inside St Mary's Church, Priory Road in 1878.

An unusual story about the Priory occurs in the State Papers of 1634-35. About the year 1595 Ferdinando Howard was married at the church in the Savoy to a young lady called Sappton, whose parents resided at Kilburn Abbey. (Kilburn Priory was then owned by Sir Arthur Atye, and the Sappton family must have been his tenants.) After the marriage the parties dined at the neighbouring 'White Hart' in the Strand, and then the brother of the bride carried her on horseback back to her father's house. The marriage turned out badly, for although it took place with the full consent of both parties and the couple lived together until they had three children, the husband deserted his wife, who was then obliged to keep a seamstress's shop in Holborn. No news was heard of the husband for eight years, and the wife then took up residence with one John Knight. This information comes from a voluntary declaration, made 38 years after the marriage by the wife's brother, William Sappton, apparently with a view to regularising the connection of his sister with John Knight.

[2] Brass tablet, thought to depict Prioress Emma de St Omer

The 'Bleeding Stone' of Kilburn

In 1817 William Atkinson, of Grove End, St John's Wood, wrote a short pamphlet entitled *'The Bleeding Stone of Kilburn'*. He said that a stone was still to be seen at a place called 'Red Barn', near St John's Wood, which was *'connected with the records of Kilburn Priory by a wild and singular legend of superstition…This stone is reported to have been brought, with others, at a remote period to this place, from the shores of Whitby in Yorkshire, by order of Stephen de Merton, for the purpose of erecting a shrine'*. Atkinson describes the large stone as having a dark reddish stain on one side and recounts a medieval story that tells of the murder of Sir Gervase de Merton by his brother Stephen for the love of Gervase's wife. The bloody deed takes place on the shores of Whitby, and Gervase's blood stains the stone. Stephen returns to Kilburn and, unable to have his way with the Lady, he throws her into a dungeon, where she dies. Later, racked with guilt, he has the remains of his brother exhumed from Whitby and buried with his wife in Kilburn, where he erects a costly shrine from stones brought from Whitby, including the Bleeding Stone on which his brother died. When he 'saw the bloody mark flow afresh and heard a groan' he fled and confessed his crime to Gilbert, Bishop of London. He then left all his lands and wealth to Kilburn Priory and became a monk. Atkinson attaches what he calls 'an old Ballad upon the subject, but evidently of a much later date, [which] testifies the existence of the legend'. This 29-verse poem tells the story in some detail.

William Atkinson was an architect who built a number of country houses, including Sir Walter Scott's 'Abbotsford'. Through the influence of Lord Mulgrave he was appointed architect to the Board of Ordnance from 1813 to 1828 and worked on the Tower of London and Woolwich Arsenal. He invented Atkinson's Cement, the raw materials of which were shipped to his wharf in Westminster from Lord Mulgrave's estates near Whitby. About 1817 Atkinson moved to a house in Grove End, St John's Wood. He lived there until about 1830, when he left for a large estate at Silvermere near Cobham in Surrey, where he died in 1839. The house in Grove End was close to Sir Edwin Landseer's house, which had been built in 1824 on the site of a property previously called Punkers Barn, or Red Barn, at the crossroads of what is now St John's Wood Road and Grove End Road.

The *Athenaeum* journal (1881) published a poem by Sir Walter Scott [3] entitled *The Muckle Stain or the Bleeding Stone of Kilburn Priory* which is reproduced in *The Priory of Kilburn* by Lady Herbert (1882). This is a slightly shorter version of the poem quoted by Atkinson in 1817, with minor differences. Extremely revealing is the introductory note from the unnamed correspondent attached to the poem:

> *My late father was a friend of Scott's, and helped him in the decoration and finishings of Abbotsford. Scott would often dine with my father when in London, and was greatly interested in the garden. In one corner there was some rockwork, in which were inserted some fragments of stone ornaments from the ruins of Kilburn Priory: and crowning all, was a large irregularly shaped stone, having a deep red stain, no doubt of ferruginous origin. This stone was sent to my father by Lord Mulgrave in one of his cement vessels, my father having been struck with its appearance on the shore at Whitby: and from these simple really unconnected facts, Scott made out the following story, in verses, which might be regarded as a kind of friendly offering in return for the services rendered.*

What can we conclude from all this? There is clearly a link between William Atkinson, Sir Walter Scott, Lord Mulgrave at Whitby, and Kilburn Priory. It seems that Atkinson, a keen geologist, took parts of the ruins for the garden of his new house in Grove

[3] (Sir) Walter Scott, at about the age he wrote the poem *The Bleeding Stone of Kilburn Priory*. Artist unknown, possibly Henry Raeburn

End about 1817. He also installed there a large stone with a red stain, which Lord Mulgrave had shipped to him from Whitby. Atkinson showed these stones to Walter Scott, and together they made up the story about Stephen and Gervase de Merton (a handwritten and dated first version by Atkinson was found in Whitby). After Scott's death in 1832 and Atkinson's death in 1839, the poem was sent for publication in the *Athenaeum* by one of Atkinson's sons (William or Henry George Atkinson). There is no trace of Stephen and Gervase de Merton (or Mertoun, Morton, Mortoune, as it appears in the various versions of the story) in any medieval references. We may conclude that Scott and Atkinson concocted the story and that it is without historical foundation.

Kilburn Wells

In the 18th century Kilburn gained a reputation among Londoners as a resort known as 'Kilburn Wells'. It grew up around a medicinal spring of fresh water in Abbey Fields, near the site of the old Kilburn Priory and in the grounds of The Bell public house [4]. In its time Kilburn Wells was almost as celebrated as Hampstead Wells. Pleasure Gardens were opened and subsequently improved by the proprietor, as shown by the following advertisement in the Public Advertiser of 17 July 1773:

> *Kilburn Wells, near Paddington. The waters now are in the utmost perfection: the gardens enlarged and greatly improved; the house and offices re-painted and beautiful in the most elegant manner. The whole is now open for the reception of the public, the great room being particularly adapted to the use and amusement of the politest companies. Fit either for music, dancing or entertainments. This happy spot is equally celebrated for its rural situation, extensive prospects, and the acknowledged efficacy of its waters; it is most delightfully situated near the site of the once famous Abbey of Kilburn, on the Edgware Road, at an easy distance, being but a morning's walk, from the metropolis, two miles from Oxford Street; the foot-way from the Mary-bone across the fields is still nearer. A plentiful larder is always provided, together with the best of wines and other liquors. Breakfasting and hot loaves.*

In 1801 Dr John Bliss carried out a series of experiments and analysed the water from both Kilburn and Hampstead Wells. Writing about Kilburn he said:

> *The spring rises about twelve feet below the surface and is enclosed in a large brick reservoir, which bears the date of 1714 on the key stone of the arch over the door. The water collected in the well is usually of the depth of five or six feet, but in a dry Summer it is from three to four, at which time its effect as a purgative is increased.... When taken fresh from the well a few inches under the surface it is tolerably clear, but not of a crystal transparency: at first it is insipid, but leaves an evident saline taste on the*

[4] The Bell, Kilburn, c.1770

tongue. *At rest, and even on slight agitation, no smell is produced but on stirring the water forcibly from the bottom of the reservoir, it becomes turbid from impurities which have been collected in it, and a considerable odour is emitted like that from the scouring of a foul gun barrel.*

Bliss said that when from one to three pints were taken at very short intervals the purgative operation was slow and gentle. He recommended it for indigestion and various other problems. The use of the water for curative purposes appears to have generally ceased in the early part of the 19th century, although it was still advertised as late as 1841. The Old Bell, or Kilburn Wells, continued to enjoy popularity as a tea garden and sometime theatre or music-hall [5] well into the 19th century.

When the London and North Western Railway was being constructed in 1838,

[5] Advertisement for entertainment at Kilburn Wells in 1821

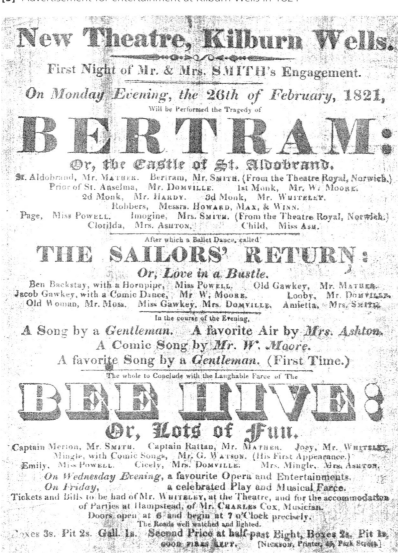

the line cut through the pleasure gardens, after which the part just behind the public house was used as a tea garden and the other part, where the well was, became a kitchen garden. Patrons of the public house had to cross the railway line at street level. In 1863 the old Bell was pulled down and the present public house was erected in its place.

The exact location of the well has long been disputed, but we now believe that it was behind the shops on the High Road, about 50 metres north of the corner of Belsize Road. In 1891, excavations for a new shop exposed *'the remains of a bricked-up arch and passage-way, and the ruins of what was once a carefully-preserved well'* next to the wall of No.46 Kilburn High Road, close to the Belsize Road corner. *'Further digging brought to view a paved way and indications of steps…Mr William Vere* [who had lived in Kilburn for many years] *is of the opinion that this was the famous well, and structural indications tally with the tradition that the well was approached from the Tea Gardens and from the road by a circular series of steps and a short passage.'* A stone plaque on the building now occupied by the health-food shop Holland and Barrett at the corner of Belsize Road claims it as the (approximate) site of Kilburn Wells.

Charles Dickens in Sketches by Boz (1836) describes a Sunday visit to 'some well-known rural Tea-gardens':

> *What a dust and noise! Men and women – boys and girls – sweethearts and married people – babies in arms, and children in chaises – pipes and shrimps – cigars and periwinkles – tea and tobacco. Some of the finery of these people provokes a smile, but they are all clean, and happy, and disposed to be good-natured and sociable.*

Kilburn Wells must have been very like this at the peak of its popularity.

Benedict Arnold's duel at Kilburn Wells

Though frowned upon by the authorities, numerous 'duels of honour' took place in the 18th Century and were well publicised; duelling was made illegal only in 1819. Duels were particularly prevalent among young military men. They often selected rural or isolated neighbourhoods just outside Town for the encounter, and 'Kilburn Wells' was a favourite venue. In 1792 Lord Lauderdale and General Arnold met here, to end a disagreement. The Earl of Lauderdale had made a slighting remark about Arnold in the House of Lords and been challenged by Arnold to a duel. In June the press wrongly reported that *'Genl. A. had been killed in a duel with the Earl of Lauderdale'*. This was incorrect, as the duel had yet to take place, at 7 am on the morning of 2 July. The protagonists agreed to fire together on command after taking their paces. Arnold fired his pistol, and although Lauderdale was unhurt, he declined to return Arnold's shot. He addressed the onlookers, saying he had not come to shoot the General, but neither could he retract the words he had used; if General Arnold was not satisfied, he might fire till he was. The seconds on being consulted declared the duel over.

The 'General Arnold' whom Lauderdale fought was in fact Benedict Arnold, notorious as 'America's first traitor'. Born in Connecticut in 1741, Arnold first trained as an apothecary and then became a Captain in the American Army in the war against the British. When George Washington suggested that Arnold lead the invasion of Canada in 1775, he was promoted to Colonel. The going was very tough, with appalling weather conditions, and Arnold failed to take Quebec. He subsequently achieved some military success but also made enemies in Congress.

In 1778 he signed the Oath of Allegiance to his country, and after the evacuation of the British in Philadelphia, Washington appointed Arnold commandant of the city. Here he met Margaret (Peggy), the beautiful young daughter of Judge Edward Shippen and they married on 8 April 1779, when she was 18 and he was a 38-year-old widower. The couple lived well beyond their means and Arnold entered into some shady deals. These included the use of government supplies for his own personal needs, for which he was court-martialled. Arnold had fought gallantly for his country and felt hurt by the way he had been treated.

He decided to approach Sir Henry Clinton, the British commander in chief in America. Money played an important part in his actions: Arnold asked Clinton for £20,000 if he was successful in betraying West Point and its garrison (where Arnold was now in command) to the British, and £10,000 if he failed. Clinton agreed to pay the first sum but only £6,000 if Arnold was unsuccessful. Arnold began correspondence with Major John Andre, Clinton's chief of intelligence. Andre was a friend of Peggy's from the time of the British occupation of Philadelphia, and recently discovered papers show that she was well aware of what her husband was doing. But the plan went wrong. Andre was captured by the Americans in September 1780 and letters from Arnold and Clinton were discovered concealed in his sock. Andre, aged 29, was tried and executed as a spy: in 1782 George III had a memorial erected to him in Westminster Abbey. Arnold managed to escape and defected to the British in New York, where he received the promised £6,000, followed by later payments from King George. In December 1781 the Arnold family sailed for England.

Arnold and Peggy arrived on 22 January 1782 and at first they were well received at court. But this soon changed and they were largely ignored, apart from a small group of American Loyalists in London. Arnold had done well from his deals and they lived in a succession of leased houses in Portman Square and Gloucester Place. Arnold, who before the Revolution had prospered as a maritime merchant, bought a brig in 1785 and sailed for St John in the Canadian province of New Brunswick. He expanded his business there but when Peggy later went to see her family in Philadelphia, she was snubbed in the streets. In 1791 the long-standing dislike of Arnold erupted and a mob overran the front lawn of his house in St John and burned an effigy of him as traitor. The couple decided to leave America and on New Year's Day 1792 they sailed for England. Arnold received favourable publicity after the duel with Lauderdale at Kilburn Wells, and again tried to get a government post. But nothing happened, and in 1794 he returned to his maritime trade. For the next two years he worked for the British in the West Indies against the French. But in 1801 he fell ill and died in London on 14 June; Peggy died three years later.

It is interesting to note that a plaque on his house at 62 Gloucester Place describes Arnold as 'American Patriot' and says he lived there from 1796 until his death in 1801.

Kilburn tollgate

The state of the Edgware Road was so 'ruinous' that in 1710 an Act of Parliament established a Turnpike Trust with powers to put up gates and tollhouses to raise money for the upkeep and repair of the road. In 1819 the toll was 2 shillings for a six-horse coach and 2d for a horse or mule. As building spread up both sides of the Edgware Road, the gates were moved progressively further north. When George Pocock began building on the Abbey Farm estate in the 1820s, its houses stood some distance north of the Pineapple Place turnpike gate, which was near the present junction with Hall Road, St John's Wood. This may have affected their saleability: contemporaries noted that because all horse-drawn traffic had to pay a toll to pass a turnpike, houses on the 'Town' or London side of any gate could generally be let more readily than those beyond. The Pineapple Place gate was removed in 1838.

What the locals called the Kilburn gate is shown in the undated photograph [6], with the toll keeper standing at the door of his booth. It stood just north of the Edgware Road junction with the road named Kilburn Priory. However, the notice on the left, which displays the rates charged, reads 'Pine Apple Gate': possibly, the road authorities recycled the board after the gate by Hall Road was removed. The building to the right is Goubert's nursery at the junction with Kilburn Priory. Beyond the toll gate, the road climbs up a slight incline towards the shops and houses of Kilburn High Road. The tollgate was removed in 1864.

[6] The Kilburn Tollgate, shortly before its removal © M Colloms

2 Development of the area up to 1846

The Abbey Farm estate was bounded on the west by Edgware Road, with the northern boundary following the line of West End Lane as far as the present Quex Road. South and east, it shared a boundary with the Eyre estate. This account is, however, concerned only with that part of the estate lying south of Belsize Road.

Tracing the development of this area has been fraught with difficulty, and there remain a number of unanswered or irresolvable questions. The property straddled the boundary between the parishes of Hampstead and St Marylebone, which caused many problems when we were tracking houses and their occupants through census and rate books. Building began in the early 1820s, when surviving parish records are poor in both volume and content. The contemporary Hampstead Vestry minutes make little or no reference to how or when roads were built, while properties are frequently described as being in 'Kilburn', without further detail. The St Marylebone rates are slightly more useful in locating properties. House numbers changed over the years, sometimes more than once. As parish and metropolitan government evolved, the legal responsibilities of landowners with regard to road building was defined, but in the early decades of the 19th century there was little formal framework. Most of the surviving records are distributed between Camden and Westminster local study archives, but many of the estate papers are still in private hands.

Colonel Fulk Greville Howard

Henry Howard was created Earl of Suffolk in 1745. When he died his estates passed to his aunt, the Hon. Frances Howard. She married Richard Bagot in 1783 and he assumed the name Howard. They had one daughter, Mary, who married the Hon. Fulk Greville-Upton on 9 July 1807, and he also changed his name to Howard. He was born in 1773, the son of Clotworthy Upton (the 1st Baron Templetown of County Antrim, Ireland). Mary inherited a considerable amount of property, amounting to over 18,000 acres of land in different parts of the country. Howard and Mary had no children, so when he died on 4 March 1846 the Kilburn estate passed to his nephew, General the Hon. Arthur Upton.

The Abbey Farm estate

Howard had bought the 40-acre Abbey Farm in 1819. As he had no obvious links with Kilburn, this was probably a speculative purchase. House building in London was on the upturn. Building was progressing in St John's Wood on the neighbouring Eyre estate, and maps of the period show the route of Abbey Road boldly striking across the fields north and east of the boundary with Abbey Farm.

Within weeks of taking possession of Abbey Farm, Howard leased two parcels of land at opposite ends of the estate to different developers. That bordering West End Lane lies outside the scope of this book. The other plot, fronting the Edgware Road close to where the Kilbourne stream crossed the main road, was leased to George Pocock, a property speculator, developer and surveyor.

Pocock set out to create an exclusive residential enclave. In 1819, Kilburn was a rural neighbourhood well north of the main built-up area of London, and eminently suitable for the development of 'country' houses for sale or rent to wealthy businessmen. In some case, families would move out of town just for the summer, and if the head of the household needed to commute, Edgware Road provided relatively rapid access into London or the City.

Pocock laid out just one road into the open fields, at right angles to the Edgware Road. In honour of the landowner this was named Greville Place, sometimes referred to as Greville Hill. For many years this road was a cul-de-sac leading nowhere and ending at or close to the parish boundary. But it pointed towards Abbey Road on the neighbouring Eyre property, so the possibility of linking the two streets was clearly in someone's mind. Pocock built houses along Greville Place and also along the Edgware Road frontage; the latter were named and numbered as 'Priory', later amended to 'Kilburn Priory'. Some semi-detached properties were described as 'two having the appearance of one', while others stood in their grounds. Most in Greville Place had their own coach house and stables.

From a point on the Edgware Road a little to the north of the Greville Place junction, another road was formed on the estate leading northwest to West End Lane. It ran close by houses on the northern plot of land Fulk Greville had leased for building. At first this road had no name, being simply described in 1833 as 'private'. A toll bar was placed across its junction with Edgware Road to prevent any unauthorised traffic using the road as a short cut north to the village of West End. It was at one time called Priory Road, but the Vestry finally sanctioned the name 'Kilburn Priory', noting its significance as one 'of local note and history'. By 1823 a house had been built on its western frontage, a little north of the Edgware Road junction, where a second house was also being built.

Howard's lawyer and agent was Thomas Hill Mortimer, a solicitor who lived in the prestigious Albany on Piccadilly. Mortimer dealt and negotiated with Pocock, and many of the surviving land and house sale details give Mortimer as the main contact.

In 1826, George Pocock's 11-year-old son John started to keep a diary, probably soon after arriving at his new Kilburn home. The boy recorded that his father moved the entire family from Holloway, 'to the fine and excellent estate of Kilburn, at the site of the old Priory'. At the outset, prospects were rosy: 'This was certainly one of the best speculations he ever made'. As was his custom elsewhere, George named his children after his latest speculation: Eliza Kilburn Pocock was born in 1819, and Lewis Greville Pocock in 1823. The first three houses (two on Edgware Road and one in Greville Place) were completed by 1822. Three years later, there were seven properties fronting Edgware Road (where Pocock's own villa was being built), a further five in Greville Place and two houses on the 'private road'. One or two houses were bought or leased by business contacts and friends of the Pocock family. Unfortunately the general economic collapse of that year cut short the metropolitan building boom, with disastrous results for Pocock. Using coded entries in his diary, John recorded that his father was experiencing financial problems. He only gives his father's side of the story; so we cannot know whether Pocock's problems were the result of his Kilburn transactions or if there was an accumulation of debts from previous speculations as well. John accused Mortimer of making loans to his father at high rates of interest 'on security which completely fettered the estate'. Eventually 'like a mercenary man, (Mortimer) refused him further assistance', so that George was sent to a debtor's prison in 1826. 'Mr Mortimer called, and Mama had some high words with him concerning the Greville Hill Estate'. While Mortimer's actions may have precipitated Pocock's imprisonment, the solicitor's responsibility was ultimately to the landowner and not to Pocock.

Building plots on Greville Place were advertised for sale in 1825 and again the following year. A sale of 300,000 bricks, in lots of five, ten or twenty thousand, plus two brick carts and two 'well known useful cart horses' was held at the Brickfield, Kilburn Priory in September 1826. The following year, in a further attempt to clear his debts, George Pocock decided to sell all his property on the estate, including his own large, newly completed three-storey house facing the main road. His son noted that a small cottage on Greville Place was to be the new family home, but George was clearly hoping to raise the maximum amount of cash, and the cottage property was included in the sale. The advertisement for Pocock's own house said:

Elegant freehold detached residence: Coach house, stabling, walled garden [at] Kilburn Priory – fine uninterrupted and picturesque views of the surrounding countryside. Recently built 5 airy bedrooms, stone steps to lobby, drawing room, breakfast and dining parlours, library.

This was No.7 Kilburn Priory, personally designed by Pocock and described by the young John as 'The best and largest house in the Priory – a perfect triumph of architecture, the envy of many of our neighbours.' He went on to recall the 'two bold front bows, and three elegant arches thrown across from the house to the stable...the semicircular drive and a large and luxurious garden behind, full of choice fruit trees and vegetables.'

John noted that his father wanted £1,900 for the family home. A neighbour made a low offer of £1,200 so George decided to keep the house, but sublet part of it. The first tenants were a married couple and then the Misses Coney took up residence and opened a school for young ladies.

Pocock also took advantage of the system whereby those who could afford it bought their way out of the King's Bench debtors' prison on a daily basis. He managed to clear some debts, and tried to 'effect a settlement with Mortimer', but his son's diary shows that the family's money problems persisted. When George Pocock died in 1829, his financial problems were largely unresolved. John was soon apprenticed to a surgeon and left England for Australia a few months later: '*I looked back upon Kilburn as long as I could catch a glimpse of the place and I never knew Kilburn look so lovely before*'. His mother Hannah remained in the family home until 1833, but by the 1841 census she was living in Margaret Street, Marylebone with five of her children, sharing the house with an artist. George's failure to leave the family in funds appears to be borne out by Hannah's occupation of 'embroideress'.

The Abbey Farm speculation may have proved a disaster for George Pocock (and provided little immediate profit for Howard), but the villas in Greville Place and along the main London Road must have contributed to the glowing description of the neighbourhood that appeared in a Directory for 1828-9:

Kilburn of late years has much increased in consequence and many beautiful villas and houses have been built around it...The pleasant distance it is from London, joined to the constant accommodation of coaches, renders it a place much frequented by opulent persons who have town residences.

At the same time, Kilburn was still far enough from London proper to be described as '*a hamlet...rural and healthy*', which reinforced the impression of Greville Place as a desirable country retreat for the wealthy.

It is possible only in general terms to date the progress of road building that followed the development of Greville Place. Common practice was for a landowner or developer to plan, excavate and lay down the line of a road. There were two major obstacles to road making on this southern part of Abbey Farm, one natural, the other man-made. The natural obstacle was the Kilbourne stream, which passed under the Edgware Road at Kilburn Bridge, to join the Westbourne and flow into the Serpentine in Hyde Park. On the Hampstead side, before it crossed the main road, it formed a large pond near the site of the old Priory. As late as 1845, the stream and pond were clearly visible on a contemporary map. The man-made obstacle – the building of the main railway line from Euston to Birmingham (the London & Birmingham, later London & North Western, Railway) – was of greater significance. Opened in 1838, it cut the property in two. All new streets would have to accommodate the rail tracks (see map on p 2).

3   Building completed

The Upton estate

After Colonel Arthur Upton inherited the Kilburn property from his uncle in 1846, the property was generally referred to as the Upton estate. The existing private road (later named Kilburn Priory) appears to have been used to divide the estate into two distinctly different areas. To the west, on the smaller triangular plot hemmed in by the railway and Edgware Road, development mainly took the form of cramped terrace housing: Upton stipulated 'close adjoining properties' of the minimum value of £200 each, and some properties backed directly on to the railway lines. In 1845, the estate had made an agreement with local builder James Carter to build Goldsmiths Place and Manchester Mews, off Edgware Road. Carter also began building along the private road, calling his houses Springfield Villas. The apex of the triangle formed by the junction of Kilburn Priory and Edgware Road was more open and was leased to a florist as a nursery ground.

In 1851, Upton obtained an Act of Parliament which resolved a problem with his uncle's will and enabled him to formally grant 99-year leases. He had already signed a provisional agreement with a developer, George Duncan, who had worked extensively on the neighbouring Eyre estate and who began developing the remaining part of the estate east of Kilburn Priory. Here the street layout was generously proportioned and until Alexandra Road was built between the railway and Mortimer Road in the late 1860s, the houses were set back some distance from the railway lines. The largest building plots were on the slightly rising ground of Greville Road and more particularly Mortimer Road, where house building on a grandiose scale occurred. These properties were developed by estate agent Ferdinand Ball and his colleague Isaac Coney, as well as by Duncan. In 1858, Ball was offering land in Mortimer Road for sale or on a 90-year lease, 'commanding delightful views' and 'only suited' for the building of villas.

Duncan was responsible for creating most if not all of the roads east of Kilburn Priory. Here the owners of the Abbey Farm/Upton property and the neighbouring St Johns Wood/Eyre estate agreed to run two roads across their joint boundary. As early as 1829 Pocock and Walpole Eyre had been in negotiation over land, Pocock wishing to fulfil his intention 'to run Greville Place Road [sic] into the Abbey Road'. However, this did not happen until the 1850s. Alexandra Road, the last to be completed, was laid down soon after 1863-4. George Duncan, who had worked on the Eyre estate, may have proposed this link to Abbey Road, but it was left to others (including his son) to execute it, as he died in 1854. The street layout was fully established by the late 1860s, when building was almost complete.

Services on the estate gradually developed. Roads remained effectively dirt tracks, and were 'paved', i.e. provided with kerbs and a hard, durable surface, only when enough houses had been built to merit it. The work was usually done by the Vestry but paid for by the land or house owners. Once completed to the Vestry's satisfaction, the road was then 'adopted' by the local authority and upkeep became the responsibility of the parish.

In summer, the unpaved streets were dusty and unpleasant and the practice of watering the road surfaces was established by the parish. The 1857 rates show that the St Marylebone parts of Edgware Road and Greville Place were 'watered' but the newly created and still building Greville and Mortimer Roads were not.

In 1854 the Hampstead Vestry had discussed adopting several of the Upton roads, as they were deemed of 'sufficient utility' to justify parish upkeep. But no action was taken, possibly because the surveyor considered some of the roads to have been poorly constructed. No further progress had been made by 1863, when Springfield Gardens and Goldsmiths Place were described as 'scarcely passable' and it was reported that most of the roads on the estate were deteriorating: '*The best property on the estate is much damaged by the approach from the Edgware-road at Kilburn gate which is flat, damp and dirty nearly all the year round*'.

The tollgate that stood across the main road at its junction with Kilburn Priory was removed the following year, together with the bar across the side road. Perhaps as part of the general improvement works, the Vestry also ordered a row of trees to be cut down, claiming they were '*neither useful or ornamental, they obscured the light and kept the road damp, and after nightfall, they were only a shelter for idle characters*'. The Hampstead Vestry agreed to pave most if not all of the roads south of the railway line, and the work was completed by 1865.

Street lighting provided by the Vestry was originally in the form of naphtha lamps. But gas mains were slowly extended, so that the Vestry agreed in 1862 to provide lamps in Springfield Road, Mortimer Road, Greville Road, Goldsmiths Place, Springfield Villas and Springfield Gardens.

Newly built houses needed to be identifiable. If a whole frontage was built up at one time, a numbering sequence could be established. Isolated groups of houses such as Pocock's Edgware Road villas might be individually named or numbered in terraces.

Poorer housing

The different policies applied over the estate gave rise to pronounced contrasts in housing. Parts of the tightly developed western triangle between Edgware Road and Kilburn Priory attracted frequent criticism. A number of properties here were used as lodgings for shop workers from the High Road, notably the large Bon Marché drapers' store [7](p 22). In some streets, houses stood cheek by jowl with stables, small industrial premises and even a cowshed on the corner of Springfield Walk and Kilburn Priory. This was still in use as late as 1872 when the Vestry received a complaint from a Mr Davis who lived opposite in Alexandra Road. The Medical Officer of Health managed 'with some explanation and patience' to convince Mr Davis that the cows were not a danger to his family's health, but acknowledged there were some grounds for complaint: '*the manure was but partially*

[7] The 'Bon Marché' on Kilburn High Road at the corner of Goldsmiths Place in 1885

removed and enough left behind to keep up a putrid smell'.

Further small terraces of properties were added here after the main spate of house building was over: Bell Terrace and Osborne Terrace, off Goldsmiths Gardens, and the Nos.1-15 (odd) on the west side of Kilburn Priory, built in the long gardens that extended back from the premises on Edgware Road. In 1868, Kilburn's first public baths [8] opened at 5 Osborne Terrace, behind the Red Lion pub. The Baths' proprietor, John Cawley, probably built all nine houses in the Terrace. The pool was small, about 30 feet long, and after a short and 'struggling existence of some dozen years' the building was permanently converted into a hall hired for various local events. Interestingly, the Tichborne Claimant sympathisers held rallies here.

Mrs Eliza Lee, from 2 Kilburn Baths, was among the day trippers missing when the 'Princess Alice' paddle boat was rammed and sunk in the Thames in September 1878. Her husband and cousin had gone home by train, but after a rail crash the week before, Eliza had decided the river trip would be safer. Her body was later identified by Alfred Ward, a 'professor of swimming' at the Baths.

In 1863, the adjacent Manchester Mews was described as being in an *'untidy and filthy state, being badly paved, badly cleansed and apparently a common receptacle for rubbish'*. Conditions were criticised again the following year. In 1875 more complaints were made by 'the inhabitants about Manchester Mews', this time supported by a certificate from two doctors and a threat to take their case to the Privy Council. The Medical Officer inspected the Mews: *'a slaughter house, cowhouse, stabling for many omnibus horses were there; much offence was given by imperfect removal of dung, and by stench needlessly offending by being taken away in the mid-day time'.* All that could be done was to recommend a notice be issued to the offending parties.

Sadly for its many residents, Goldsmiths Place frequently featured in the reports made by the Medical Officer of Health (MOH) for Hampstead. In 1859 he complained of the road's *'abominable basements'* and in 1863 he noted that illness *'still prevailed'* in and around the street. Mains drainage was provided by January 1866 but in August the MOH commented on the poor sanitary arrangements that still existed. When a child died of scarlet fever in 1876, the MOH's report noted the disease had been *'rife'* in the road and criticised the overcrowded and unsanitary conditions prevailing among the properties. In March 1878, another death occurred, this time a 6-month-old baby living at No.1 Goldsmiths Gardens, who had been suffering from diphtheria, and in May the MOH reported the disease was *'still hanging about Belsize Road and Kilburn'*. In 1882, he was pressing for the owners of Nos.2, 3, 4, 5 and 6 to provide a new drain to the public sewer, as the present outlet was blocked. Between them these five houses showed a total of 81 people as resident on census night 1881, with 25 persons living in No.2 alone.

This area became even more congested with the loss of the nursery ground, by then known as Goubert's, and the building of a terrace of eight houses on Kilburn Priory, at the end of gardens that originally reached back from houses on the High Road. These houses, Nos.1–15 (odd), were completed by 1891.

House styles in the roads east of Kilburn Priory were more varied. They ranged from large detached mansions in Mortimer Road to the more formulaic Victorian houses of Alexandra Road and neighbouring streets and the older, Georgian-style properties in Greville Place. During the 1850s, some of the largest houses on the estate were built on slightly elevated land in Mortimer Road. Known as North Hall, Harlestone Villa, Mount Greville, St John's Hall and Mayfield, these are described in greater detail in Chapter 7.

Social and commercial life

Almost from the outset the residents' material needs were well catered for by the shops and traders on either side of Kilburn High Road, which rapidly developed into a major retail area. Their spiritual needs were also attended to and John Pocock's diary recalls a great day in the life of the district:

March 1st 1829: Sunday. Our new Chapel opened this day [on the site of the present Kilburn Square]. *The little village of Kilburn never looked so lively or proud as on this day. We had an excellent sermon adapted to the occasion by the Rev'd Mr Hancock who is appointed minister. Altogether it will be a very great blessing to the place and is likely to enhance the value of all the property in the neighbourhood.*

KILBURN BATHS
5, OSBORNE TERRACE,
Nearly opposite the Cambridge Road,
HIGH ROAD, KILBURN.

PRIVATE HOT & COLD BATHS.

Cold & Tepid Shower & Swimming Baths.

TERMS TO THE
WARM BATHS
1st CLASS.

Private Warm Bath	£0	1	0
Twelve Tickets	0	9	0

2nd CLASS.

Warm Bath	0	0	6
Tepid or Cold Shower Bath...	£0	0	8
Twelve Tickets	0	6	0

OPEN ON SUNDAYS UNTIL 9 O'CLOCK, A.M.

THE
SWIMMING BATH
Open from April 1st to October 31st.

A Single Ticket ... £0 0 8	Two Months £0 15 0
Twelve Tickets ... 0 7 0	Three Months ... 0 17 6
One Month 0 10 6	The Season 1 1 0

FIRST & SECOND CLASS PRIVATE BATHS FOR LADIES', TERMS AS ABOVE.

ARRANGEMENTS MADE WITH SCHOOLS.
J. CAWLEY Proprietor.

[8] Advertisement for Kilburn Baths, 5 Osborne Terrace.

At a time when most people attended a service at least once on Sunday, a local church was seen as important in securing the future of an estate. But for the next 30 years, Kilburn residents had to look further afield for such ceremonies as marriages and christenings, as the Kilburn chapel was not consecrated. The developer George Duncan reserved a site at the corner of Abbey and Priory Roads to build a church to serve the entire estate. However, this plan lay dormant until an upturn in building meant that pews would soon be filled. In June 1856 *The Times* carried a list of the people who had given money for the church building appeal, many of whom were wealthy local residents. Colonel Upton was invited to lay the foundation stone, and St Mary's opened the following year. From 1880, residents could also choose to attend the High Church services at St Augustine's, across the Edgware Road.

Non-conformists were also catered for: the Greville Place Congregational Church opened in 1859. From the mid-1860s, No.1 Greville Road was home to a small group of Catholic priests newly arrived in the neighbourhood, and for several years it served as both presbytery and church. 'It was so small that the people had to enter and leave in tiny separate groups', until the large Sacred Heart church in Quex Road opened in 1879. A synagogue also opened at the corner with Harrow Road in 1863 and the St John's Wood Synagogue, Abbey Road, opened in 1882.

Upton took the unusual decision to encourage the building of a local station. This opened in 1852 on Belsize Road with trains running to Euston, but for many years the service was patchy. The horse buses on nearby Edgware Road carried far more of the residents to their work in London.

Booth's *Survey of London* (1889) reveals no great surprises, the wealthiest residents being found in the more spacious streets east of Kilburn Priory, notably Mortimer Road, Greville Place and Greville Road. Between the time of the survey and WW I, the impression is one of a mixed area: large, singly occupied houses, with others split between several families. There was a commensurate cross-section of residents, ranging from independently wealthy men and women, to professional types (in particular, a large complement of solicitors), and workers drawn from almost every possible field. The occupants of the large Mortimer Road and Greville Place houses were mostly wealthy men from various commercial backgrounds. A particular feature of the neighbourhood from the late 19th century onwards was the large number of artists it attracted. Property was cheaper than in neighbouring St John's Wood, sometimes referred to as the 'abode of the arts'; Greville Road and Greville Place were favoured streets for establishing studios. When one artist left, another would often take his or her place. The turnover of residents reflected the fact that until the middle of the 20th century, renting or short-lease accommodation was far more usual than freehold purchase.

Over the years these streets also housed a variety of scholastic, philanthropic or medical/institutional enterprises. Most were short-lived, occupying a single terrace house, but others, notably the St Peter's Home for the 'respectable' sick and dying, occupied two of the largest properties in Mortimer Road and was still functioning in the 1940s. Of the schools, which were usually dedicated to single-sex education, perhaps the best known was Henley House, also in Mortimer Road.

4 Redevelopment

The first major change occurred in the mid-1850s, when the substantial Pocock mansion in Kilburn Priory was divided and remodelled to provide three separate houses: later numbered as 132, 134 and 136 Maida Vale. The properties immediately to the north – Nos.140 and 138 Maida Vale – stood on two of the largest plots on the estate. They were both demolished during the opening decades of the 20th century, and their sites were used for a cinema and a fire station, the latter soon converted into the local Maida Vale telephone exchange, which opened in 1922.

After WWI, some of the streets continued to decline. Here, properties had been poorly built, rented out and badly maintained from the start. It was also becoming harder and more expensive to run some of the larger houses in the better streets as single homes, and many were subdivided into flats. The disposal of freeholds meant there was no large 'falling in' of leases and the associated chance for an individual to remodel the area, while local authorities lacked the power to do more than urge landlords to make basic repairs. Overall, however, this enclave appears to have retained a mixture of residents drawn from all walks of life, right up to the outbreak of war in 1939 and in some cases beyond.

Another way of making money from property in this and other London neighbourhoods where there were old houses on big plots became widespread in the 1930s. Hampstead Council received numerous applications for Kilburn and West Hampstead from speculators who bought houses with the intention of demolishing them and redeveloping their sites as blocks of flats. The Upton estate, with its generous layout and spacious villas, was a prime target, with early attention focused on Mortimer Place and Mortimer Crescent. In 1933 Hampstead Council considered a proposal to demolish North Hall and replace it with seven smaller houses. The LCC felt *'the erection of houses on this site was preferable to the erection of flats'*, and Hampstead Council reluctantly agreed, but the house survived as a private residence for another decade. Despite the LCC's comment, many people had come to view flat dwelling as a convenient way to live. An apartment block could be scaled to fit many situations – to replace a single house on a big plot, or a group of houses, or even one of a semi-detached pair of houses (see below)! Some observers feared that without regulation Hampstead would be swamped by apartment blocks. After a discussion by the Council in 1934, Dr Lewis Glover wrote to the local newspaper deploring the apparently 'insatiable demand' for flats in Hampstead. His comments have particular relevance for the Upton estate:

> When a likely private house with a garden behind it comes on the market the 'speculative builder' comes forward with his friends and seeks authority to pull down the building and cover the ground with bricks and mortar; so that where there was one building with open space around it, there spring up blocks of flats, trees and shrubs are cut down and the amenities of the surrounding properties are destroyed.

1933 saw the building of a large block of 122 residential flats that epitomised 'convenience' living. Hillsborough Court replaced a single property, the 1860s Mayfield (Cottage) set in a large plot of land with frontages to Mortimer Place, Mortimer Crescent and Alexandra Road. And in 1939, Ascot Lodge at the corner of Greville Road and Greville Place was completed, a block of 15 flats replacing Nos.9 and 11 Greville Place.

Two of the oldest properties on the estate – the original Nos.1 and 2 Kilburn Priory, later Nos.120 and 122 Maida Vale – came under threat in 1936. More accurately, the proposal directly affected only No.122. It was reported that a developer intended to demolish the house *'to make way for yet another block of flats'*. As this pair was among the original 'two having the appearance of one' houses, clearly the loss of the mirror property would have a huge effect on No.120. It was said that its owner had agreed to sell to the developers, but the price offered was too low for him to accept. A description of what happened next depended on the viewpoint of the writer. Conservationists argued that the villas were among the oldest houses in the area, their attractive façade making a positive contribution to the neighbourhood. Modernists spoke of *'stucco-fronted villas standing in long front gardens and looking very shabby…but even these are slowly giving way to new blocks of flats'*. The demolition went ahead *'to the great indignation of the owner of the surviving house'* and Greville Hall – yet another block of flats – was completed that year. The Ordnance Survey in 1937 shows the block wrapping round the corner with Greville Place, having absorbed the sites of No.2 Greville Place as well as Nos.122–126 Maida Vale. The half villa remained, until bomb damage during WW II forced its subsequent redevelopment as (predictably) a small block of flats called Carlton Court.

Attempts were made to upgrade the neighbourhood's status by claiming affiliation with St John's Wood rather than Kilburn, always known to contain a large number of working-class residents. As early as 1863 a house in Greville Place was described as being *'on the verge of St John's Wood'*. In 1939, A A Milne revisited the neighbourhood where he had spent many years as a child: *'In those days (1880s) it was Mortimer Road, Kilburn, and none the worse for that; now it is become more respectable (or Kilburn less) and is known as Mortimer Crescent, St John's Wood'*.

Hillsborough Court was advertised as being in Maida Vale, just 'three quarters of a mile from Lords Cricket Ground'. Greville Hall was advertised as 'St John's Wood'. It could be argued that by replacing old, possibly dilapidated properties, the new blocks of flats were an instrument of positive change and renewal. However, as these were all private initiatives they did not address the problems of overcrowding for tenants in the area who could not afford higher rents.

Effects of two World Wars

Because it was close to several railway lines, the Upton estate suffered bomb damage during both World Wars. Sir Francis Oppenheimer recalled a visit to James Garvin one Sunday night in 1918. He arrived about 9 pm and later that evening:

The maroons went off announcing an air raid.….Bombs began to burst in rapid succession. To judge from the violence of their explosion they were dropping none too far away. Anti-air-raid guns had come into action; shrapnel from our barrage was dropping about the house, which stood in its own grounds with a glass dome over the hall, the panes of which were shaking. … The air raid was a nerve-racking, noisy affair, stretching over hours. When at last the 'all-clear' had sounded it was immediately followed by another air-raid warning, as a single enemy raider was still caught within our barrage. It was long, very long after midnight when I left Kilburn on my dark walk back to the Ritz. I had to find my way round the first bomb crater at the corner of Greville Place and the Edgware Road. There was much similar damage and destruction upon the whole upper reaches of the Edgware Road. Willesden Junction, it was believed, had been one of the German targets.

A number of bombs hit the area during WW II, although this was far from being the most badly damaged part of Hampstead. Greville Place was hit on 18 September 1940 and again on 29 June 1944. Greville Road was damaged by four attacks on 18 September, 8 and 16 October 1940, and again on 29 June 1944. These last three attacks also caused damage in Kilburn Priory, where Nos.21 and 23 were so badly damaged that the site had to be cleared. The site of one of the High Explosive bombs which landed at the rear of No.10 Kilburn Priory on 16 October 1940 was reopened in March 1942 in order to examine the unexploded bomb. The bomb disposal squad decided it was safe at the time, but nearly 7 years later, in February 1949, the squad returned, to blow it up underground.

North Hall in Mortimer Crescent was all but destroyed at 7.50 am on 29 June 1944 by a VI flying bomb (one of ten that fell in Hampstead during the War). The Camden History Society's *Hampstead at War* notes that:

> *A flying bomb came in from the east and when over the Kilburn area made a left turn, completed a circle, then proceeded south to drop in the garden at the back of North Hall, Mortimer Crescent. Fourteen people were taken to hospital and twenty were slightly injured. North Hall, used by the Council for storing furniture belonging to people whose homes had been destroyed, was badly damaged.*

An influx of refugees plus bomb damage exacerbated conditions on the Upton estate. All the redevelopment so far had been for the benefit of private tenants, but many residents were living in overcrowded and unsanitary conditions. There was a real lack of good affordable family accommodation throughout the Kilburn Ward.

The postwar period

Soon after the end of WW II, Hampstead Borough Council and the London County Council began planning the demolition and rebuilding of much of the Kilburn Priory area. Almost all the original properties south of the railway line were progressively demolished. The major alteration to the street layout involved Alexandra Road, which became a short cul-de-sac terminating at its junction with Mortimer Crescent.

The street with the largest number of surviving houses is Greville Place. Other isolated groups of villas remain in Langtry Road (formerly Alexandra Road), Mortimer Crescent and Greville Road, and a few original houses survive behind the High Road. The pre-war spate of flat building, and the Council's post-war programme of continued redevelopment, have together largely obliterated the neighbourhood's character. Most recently, the construction of a large hotel (currently the London Marriott Maida Vale) and more residential flats prompted a second redevelopment of the triangular site at the junction of Kilburn Priory and Maida Vale and a further loss of a 19th-century terrace.

At the end of 1946, Hampstead Council sought to buy and redevelop 2.3 acres of land in the neighbourhood, in two sections. The Kilburn Priory scheme, or as it was renamed the Kilburn Gate scheme, started with the demolition of Nos.2-12 (even) Kilburn Priory, their sites being used for 60 flats; the second involved Nos.14-20 (even) Kilburn Priory and Nos.6-10 (even) Greville Road, to provide a further 34 flats. Work began on Phase 1 at the end of 1948, with Phase 2 some 4 years later. The first 60 flats were available in 1951, the remainder completed in 1957.

In 1948 the LCC began clearing the substantial area lying between Greville Road, Mortimer Place and Mortimer Crescent, where the 1944 flying bomb had done significant damage. This became the Mortimer Estate, eight blocks containing 165 flats, with two of the blocks built on the east side of Mortimer Crescent. Seven were complete by July 1953. In 1952, a further area of demolitions was planned. Just under an acre of land was involved, the sites of Nos.17-35 Kilburn Priory, two houses in Springfield Lane and premises in Springfield Walk. Fifty flats were proposed and 43 were under construction in 1954.

In 1958 yet more houses in this area were described by the Council as 'unfit for human habitation' and 'dangerous to the health of the inhabitants'. Nos.9-25 (odd) Springfield Lane and No,1 Springfield Walk were specifically mentioned. Within a few years demolition had cleared the site at the corner of these roads. The houses were replaced with a 9-storey block providing homes for 24 families at a cost of £73,000. The work was scheduled to start in 1962 and the result was Falcon House, complete by 1970. Falcon House together with the 1952 blocks on the other side of Springfield Walk now make up the Goldspring Estate. The last block was Philip House, occupying a site bordered by Kilburn Priory, Langtry Road and Mortimer Place. Because of the provision of social housing and a general decline in population, overcrowding in Kilburn Ward was greatly reduced between 1955 and 1971.

Private redevelopment took out three of the last four remaining villas on Maida Vale, Nos.128-134, and in their place stands Vivian Court, an 8-storey block of flats. Amazingly, one house survived until 1997, the much damaged and altered 'third' of Pocock's original substantial Kilburn Priory mansion, then No.136 Maida Vale. The fact that it carried a blue plaque [9] to film pioneer Friese-Greene (see p 36) delayed its final demise but ultimately did not prevent Camden Council giving permission for its demolition, despite many attempts to save it. It will come as no surprise to find that it was replaced by a small block of flats.

A modern map gives no hint of what the Upton estate was like before any redevelopment occurred. The relationship of the individual houses and terraces

[9] The Friese-Greene house, No.136 Maida Vale, shortly before demolition

to their large gardens has been destroyed, and in places even the road plan and features of local topography have been swept away. Of the few original properties that survive, many have been altered, subdivided or are hidden behind high walls. The 50-inch OS maps of the 1860s show large houses, carriage drives, big gardens, trees and ornamental planting. Today a visitor to Greville Place and the immediate area near its junction with Greville Road and Mortimer Crescent can get some idea of the neighbourhood's original character, but it takes a vivid imagination. Old cobble stones still cover the roadway of the bridge over the railway line, and the nature reserve behind No.1a Greville Place is more evocative. A handful of the remaining original properties (many subdivided into flats) are now Listed buildings; the remains of the cowshed complex opposite Langtry Road are not!

For sketch map of the estate in 2006 see inside back cover

5 Kilburn Priory and Maida Vale

n this chapter and those that follow, individual houses in each road are described, with biographies of some of the more interesting occupants. Houses are referred to by their current numbering, together with any previous numbers. For relevant maps with individually numbered houses, see pp 30 and 42.

KILBURN PRIORY

The first name given to Pocock's houses on Edgware Road was simply 'Priory' but this was soon expanded to 'Kilburn Priory'. The road leading north from Edgware Road over the railway to Belsize Road is shown as 'Priory Road' on the 1868 OS map, but this name does not appear in other records. All references to houses numbered as 'Kilburn Priory' after 1868 refer to premises in this last-named road, as the Edgware Road houses were then given numbers in Maida Vale. All the original houses in Kilburn Priory have been demolished.

The *East Side* comprised
Nos.120-140 Maida Vale, originally 1-10 consec Kilburn Priory, with some number duplication
Nos.2-26 Kilburn Priory, originally 10-19 consec Kilburn Priory; Trouville House and York House

The *West Side* comprised
Nos.1-15 odd and 17-35 odd, originally 9-18 consec Springfield Villas.

EAST SIDE (see map on p 30)
Nos.120 and 122 Maida Vale, previously Nos.1 and 2 Kilburn Priory [10]
were built by William Jefferys, a plumber of Regent Street and John Langdon, a surveyor from St Pancras. Langdon lived in No.2 Kilburn Priory for a couple of years but sold No.1 to Thomas Dickins for £1,664. Langdon may have been an associate of George Pocock's and his name crops up in his son John's diary.

Nos.120-140
Maida Vale (1868)

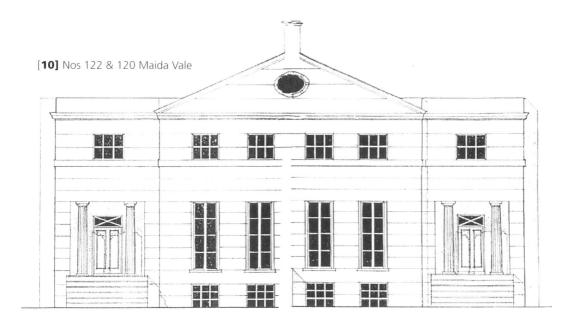

No.120 Maida Vale, previously No.1 Kilburn Priory

Thomas Dickins, linen draper, founder of Dickins and Jones, d. 1856

Dickins was probably the first occupant of this house in 1823, and he remained there until his death in 1856. Born in Lincolnshire, Thomas was a linen draper. He opened a shop in Oxford Street with William Smith in about 1803 and they used a golden lion as their trading sign. About 1827, a third partner, Joseph Stevens, joined the firm, which moved to 232 Regent Street in 1835. Dickins' two younger sons (Charles John and Henry Francis, see No.14 Greville Place) took over the business when Thomas died and created Dickins and Jones, taking on John Jones as a partner. The shop expanded and diversified, and by 1895 there were 200 staff. In 1914 Harrods acquired a controlling interest in the company, which later became part of the House of Fraser. The Regent Street store closed in 2006.

After Thomas' death, the house was advertised for sale in 1857, when it was described as being in the 'rural village of Kilburn'.

Sir Edward German (born German Edward Jones), composer, 1862–1936

Sir Edward's association with the neighbourhood was a brief one. He is shown in the 1891 census lodging at No.1 Kilburn Priory at the age of 29, when he described himself as a 'musical composer'. By 1895, he had moved up the road to No.13, and in 1905 he was living in Hall Road, St John's Wood. Born in Whitchurch, Shropshire, Edward first studied engineering, but showing great musical ability he enrolled at the Royal Academy of Music in 1880. At this time he gave up the surname of Jones because two other students had the same name. German's first symphony was performed in 1887 and he subsequently gained recognition for his incidental music for theatrical productions (including a commission from Henry Irving), which became enormously popular. He wrote several operettas and in 1911 composed the coronation march and hymn for King George V and Queen Mary. German was knighted in 1928. His music fell out of favour but *The Times* obituary acknowledged his talent, calling him

An artist of genius. The kind of music in which German excelled is commonly called 'light music', and its composer is apt to be lightly regarded. German delighted in his gift of shapely melody, and was content with the simple harmony and translucent orchestration which belongs naturally to such melody. He had no use for complexity in music, which seemed to him to be merely another word for ugliness.

He died of cancer at his home No.5 Biddulph Road, Maida Vale, in 1936.

Henry Festing Jones, musician, and biographer of Samuel Butler, 1851–1928

In 1902 Henry Festing Jones bought the freehold of 120 Maida Vale and he stayed there until his death in 1928. He was born in Gloucester Terrace in 1851, the son of Thomas Jones, QC. He obtained his degree from Cambridge and practised as a solicitor in London from 1876 to 1887. He met the writer Samuel Butler (author of *Erewhon* and *The Way of All Flesh*) in 1876 and they became intimate friends. Butler persuaded Jones to give up the law and become his musical and literary companion. He paid Jones an allowance of £200 per annum between 1887 and 1900. Butler died in June 1902 at 'Clumber House', 34 St John's Wood Road, and bequeathed £500 to Jones. Jones became Butler's biographer, publishing his notebooks in 1912 and a memoir in 1919. In February 1922 he gave a talk on Butler at Hampstead Town Hall. Jones also published books on his travels with Butler in Italy and he wrote musical pieces, including a comic opera, *King Bulbous*. Between 1902 and 1914 he organised the Erewhon literary dinners in memory of Butler. Jones was once rather happily compared to a gondola,

the motion of which, however slow, is invariably soothing and comfortable; but on the intellectual side he was not only a thoroughly competent writer and musician but also possessed an abundance of shrewdness and common sense.

He died at his house in Maida Vale in October 1928, aged 77.

No.122 Maida Vale, previously No.2 Kilburn Priory

In the 1930s, Nos.120 and 122 Maida Vale were the subject of several articles when it was proposed to demolish No.122. They were an example of several Pocock semi-detached properties on the estate with the description 'two houses with the appearance of one' (see Chapter 4, p 26).

Nos.124 and 126 Maida Vale, previously Nos.3 and 4 Kilburn Priory may have been built by James Banting, a carpenter of Cumberland Street, who went bankrupt in 1822.

No.124 Maida Vale, previously No.3 Kilburn Priory

Captain John Maples, Royal Navy, 1770–1847

John Fordyce Maples was the first occupant of this house, in 1821. Maples was born in 1770 in Colchester. When he was 12 years old Captain Philip Affleck appointed him as a captain's servant aboard his ship the 'Triumph', a 74-gun battleship. This was the start of Maples' long naval career.

In 1789 Midshipman Maples was sent to the West Indies for what turned out to be an eventful 11 years. In 1792 he returned to England to pass his exam for lieutenant, but as he lacked the family connections for rapid promotion he returned to Jamaica. Maples served under several influential captains and developed a reputation as a promising young officer. In 1793 the French declared war on England: this offered the prospect of prize money and promotion to officers like

Maples. He was soon in action on the frigate 'Penelope', where as master's mate he shared one-eighth of the bounty with twelve officers. The capture of numerous ships over the years made him quite wealthy.

In 1801 Maples was posted to the 'London', Sir Hyde Parker's flagship, which was to lead an expedition of 50 ships to the Baltic. Horatio Nelson in the 'St George' joined the squadron in March. During the successful Battle of Copenhagen at the beginning of April, Maples volunteered to serve on one of Nelson's battleships.

In September 1805 Maples was first lieutenant on the frigate 'Naiad' which joined Nelson's forces off Cadiz. During the Battle of Trafalgar, 'Naiad' was ordered to take the disabled British battleship 'Belleisle' in tow. At the same time she put boats into the water to rescue sailors from the French battleship 'Achilles' which was on fire and suddenly blew up. Despite heavy seas and the snapping of the tow cable, 'Naiad' managed to get the 'Belleisle' back to Gibraltar. They were the first ships from the battle to reach the Rock and were given a rapturous salute from the guns of the garrison. Maples, like all the other lieutenants at Trafalgar, received prize money of £65 and a government grant of £161. However, the really important reward of promotion was reserved for the officers engaged in the 'muzzle to muzzle' part of the battle, and first lieutenants of the frigates like the 35-year-old Maples were not promoted.

His luck changed in 1810, when at the fifth anniversary of Trafalgar the Lords of the Admiralty promoted 20 senior lieutenants, and Maples was made a commander and captain of a bomb vessel. Two years later, at the beginning of the war with America (November 1812), he was assigned to the command of the newly built brig 'Pelican'. In July 1813 Maples was under sail, looking for American privateers. The American brig 'Argus', captained by Henry Allen, had sailed from France on 20 July. When she reached Penzance on the 25th the Admiralty realised that instead of privateers they had a heavily armed, fast, American brig-of-war loose in the shipping lanes. At dawn on 14 August 1814 the 'Pelican' and 'Argus' sighted each other off St David's Head. The 'Pelican's' guns blasted the 'Argus', and in 45 minutes the battle was over. Captain Allen was hit by a 32-pound shot just above the knee. Of about 125 sailors aboard, six were killed in the battle and another six died later from their wounds. Allen's leg was amputated but he died of fever and was buried with full military honours in St Andrew's Church, Plymouth. The 'Pelican' sustained little damage, with only two fatalities and five wounded among the crew.

It is somewhat ironic that in death Allen was given full recognition, while Maples, the victor, was just put on half-pay to await another appointment. He wrote to the Admiralty in November 1813 from 34 Canterbury Place, Lambeth, asking about progress. Over a year later, in September 1814, he was given command of a sloop, but ill health prevented him taking up the offer. Then in December he joined another 21-gun sloop, but after putting to sea on 9 January 1815 they had sailed only a few miles before returning to shore, because Maples was too ill to continue. He was probably suffering from recurring bouts of malaria, which ended his 30-year career at sea. Maples retired on half-pay of £189 a year, but he had saved most of his prize money and knew that he if he lived long enough, he would be promoted to the rank of Rear Admiral. In 1815, commissioned officers like Maples who had been mentioned by name in dispatches in the London Gazette were made Commanders of the Bath (CB).

On 27 April 1814 John Maples married Mary Carthew, a widow of Woodbridge, Suffolk. Her first husband was John Carthew, a solicitor; they had no children, nor did she and Maples. They moved to the new house in Kilburn, where they remained until Maples' death. About 1835 Maples went blind and was cared for by a servant called Sarah Ann Coolbear, who had been with him since 1830. On 1 October 1846 the Admiralty finally promoted Maples to Rear Admiral (retired). He died less than a year later on the 12 May 1847 at No.3 Kilburn Priory, aged 78, the cause of death given as 'gradual decay'. His obituary in *The Times* noted that he had taken part in over 100 naval engagements and described him as 'a brave and truly good officer and man'.

John George Swindell, architect, d. 1850

Swindell was an architect living at No.11 Kilburn Priory in 1847, but by 1850 he had moved to No.3. In February his son was born there. Swindell's career came to an end when in May of the same year he died at Clifton, 'to the inexpressible grief of his family', aged just 25.

No.126 Maida Vale, previously No.4 Kilburn Priory

The Misses Giblett's school

The unusually named Miss Sophia and Frances Giblett ran one of the neighbourhood's earliest private boarding school for girls from 1826 at this address until 1828, when they moved round the corner to larger premises, Nos.12 and 13 Greville Place.

Greville Hall

Nos.122-126 Maida Vale and No.2 Greville Place were demolished, and their site was redeveloped as a 4-storey block of flats, Greville Hall, which was completed in 1937 and is still standing. The block was marketed as offering
  'The best value in St John's Wood. Charming new flats with large well lighted rooms, at very moderate rentals. Surrounded by gardens and trees, central heating, constant hot water, lifts, porters, excellent fitted kitchens and bath rooms.'
It is reported that the first meeting of Amnesty International took place in Mr Hassan's flat at Greville Hall in 1961.

(here is Greville Place)

No.128 Maida Vale, previously No.5 Kilburn Priory

Sarah Garrard, widow of jeweller Robert Garrard

In 1823 the first occupant of this newly completed house was Sarah Garrard, widow of Robert Garrard, the goldsmith and jeweller. She lived there only briefly, as she died the following year. Garrards was the well-established firm in Panton Street that later became the Queen's jewellers. Robert Garrard had joined the firm in 1792 and on his death his three sons took over. In 1862 they were asked to re-cut the Koh-i-Noor ('Mountain of Light') diamond from India. This massive stone was given to Queen Victoria by the East India Company in 1850 and it was displayed at the 1851 Crystal Palace Exhibition. Although it was extremely large, its lacklustre colour caused some negative comment and it was decided to have it re-cut. Garrards were entrusted with the delicate task. Although recently taken over by Asprey's, Garrards continue to be the Crown jewellers to this day.

Arthur Sidney Potter, solicitor

Solicitors Arthur Sidney Potter and then Arthur Cyril Potter were at this address from at least 1918 (Arthur Sidney moved here from No.126). The firm's office was previously at No.70 Kilburn High Road, on the corner of West End Lane. Arthur Sidney was the son of Thomas Potter, who established an iron foundry near West End Green and lived for many years in nearby Poplar House. Arthur Sidney drew up leases and other agreements for the Potters when they sold off their West Hampstead estates for building. His sister married Henry Saxon Snell (see No.3 Greville Place, p 53). The firm was still trading from 128 Maida Vale in 1970.

Nos.132, 134 and 136 Maida Vale, previously No.7 Kilburn Priory, then divided into Nos.7, 8 and 9 Kilburn Priory

George Pocock and John Chapman

The original house was constructed to George Pocock's design for his own occupation and was building in 1824 and 1825. His son called it the 'best and largest house' on the estate, but Pocock's financial problems forced the family to let part of the property almost as soon as it was completed. George Pocock died in 1829 and the family had left Kilburn by 1834. The size of the house attracted John Chapman, who named it 'Priory House' and set up a boys' school there by 1839. The 1841 census showed 19 boarding pupils aged between eight and fifteen. Chapman left about 1850 and the house was subdivided about this time to make three separate homes.

No.132 Maida Vale, previously No.7 Kilburn Priory

James Henry Goetze 1823–1877, and his son Sigismund Goetze 1866–1939

James Goetze, a colonial broker, lived at 7 Kilburn Priory from at least 1853 to 1859. His wife Eliza died at the house in September 1853, but in the 1861 census James was shown at No.13 Upper Hamilton Terrace. He died in 1877 and is buried in Paddington Cemetery, Willesden Lane. His son was Sigismund Goetze, artist, philanthropist and patron of the arts. Sigismund and his wife Constance lived at Grove House (later Nuffield Lodge) in Regent's Park from 1907. The stables were converted into an artist's studio. The couple hosted many charitable events in their garden, and made generous gifts to enhance the park: the iron gates leading to the Inner Circle in 1935 and the Triton Fountain a year later. Goetze painted a series of murals to enliven the Foreign Office in London. They took 7 years to complete, depict Britannia in a series of mythological settings, and were a gift from the artist.

Sir William Goscombe John's 1938 portrait of Sigismund Goetze hangs in the Fitzwilliam Museum, Cambridge. He attended Goetze's funeral, accompanied by neighbour Gilbert Bayes. The Goetze family grave in Paddington Cemetery is Listed Grade II.

Leslie Isaac Hore-Belisha, 1st Baron Hore-Belisha, politician, 1893–1957

Leslie was born at No.7 Kilburn Priory on 7 September 1893, the only son of Captain Jacob and Elizabeth Belisha. His father's family were Sephardic Jews who settled in Manchester. Less than a year after Leslie was born, Jacob died suddenly while preparing to go on parade with the Royal Fusiliers. Elizabeth soon left Kilburn for Pembridge Villas in Kensington. She was a devoted mother, and apparently delayed remarrying until 1912, when she married civil servant (Sir) Charles Fraser Adair Hore. At her request, Leslie added his stepfather's name to his own. Shortly before she died in 1936, Elizabeth said of her son: 'He has always said that I was his inspiration, but I can safely say that he has been mine'.

Leslie went to Oxford to read law, but his studies were interrupted by WW I, when he served in the army in Europe. Shortly after being called to the Bar in 1922 he fought a by-election at Devonport, where he stood as a Liberal. He canvassed from an old stage coach, hired for the occasion, attracting crowds by blowing a post-horn. Defeated by the incumbent Tory MP, Leslie stood at the 1923 General Election and this time took the seat, holding it until 1945. This was the start of a distinguished political career that included Ministerial and Cabinet posts.

As Secretary of State for War in the years immediately preceding the outbreak of WW II, Hore-Belisha made sweeping, positive changes to army practice and introduced partial conscription. His actions met with hostility from senior officers, and he also encountered some anti–Semitic opposition. Hore-Belisha resigned from the Government in 1940 after Chamberlain suggested that he transfer to the Board of Trade. Married in 1944, he was created a baron in 1954. Three years later, Hore-Belisha was giving a speech in Reims and had just begun to praise Anglo-French relations, when he suffered a stroke and died instantly.

His name has passed into the language from his time as Minister of Transport (1934-7), when he introduced several measures to cut the rising number of road accidents. These included pedestrian crossings marked by illuminated amber globes mounted on black and white striped metal posts which came to be called 'Belisha Beacons'. Jokes were made on radio and in music halls about the globes, while the beacons attracted much unwanted attention: in November 1934, the local paper noted the theft of eight 'beacons' close to Hore-Belisha's birthplace – from crossings in Abbey Road, Quex Road and West End Lane. A man was arrested in the act of removing one of the globes and taken to court. The magistrate seemed genuinely perplexed, asking the accused if he had a use for the globe at home! The offender was fined 40 shillings with 30 shillings costs. A marching song entitled 'Good Old Hore Belisha' was published in the year he became Secretary of State for War. The bizarre cover for the music showed a battlefield crossed by barbed wire, flanked on one side by a traffic light, and on the other, a Belisha Beacon! More positively, in 1938 a new public house in Rainham Mark, Kent was given the name 'The Belisha Beacon'.

Nos.128–134 were demolished and their sites used, together with No.1a Greville Place, for a block of flats, Vivian Court.

No.136 Maida Vale, previously No.9 Kilburn Priory

John Pepper was probably the first occupant, when he called the property 'Morton House'. He ran a tutorial business from the house: *'John H. Pepper, FCSA. Inst C.E. late Professor of Chymistry [sic] Royal Polytechnic. Receives resident or other pupils: scientific portion of the Civil Service and Military Examinations.'* (1861)

William Friese-Greene, cinema pioneer, 1855–1921
Friese-Greene rented 136 Maida Vale from 1888 to 1891. Born in Bristol in 1855 as William Edward Green, he was one of the seven children of James Green, a metalworker and goldsmith. William left school when he was 14 years old and

began an apprenticeship with local photographer Marcus Guttenberg (whose son Charles Marcus Guttenberg, also a photographic artist, committed suicide in Kilburn in 1896). In 1874 the 18-year-old William Green opened his own studio and in the same year, he married Swiss-born Victoria Mariana Helena Friese. He thought that Green was too plain a name so he added her name and called himself Friese-Greene.

Friese-Greene did well as a photographer and opened shops in Bristol, Plymouth and Bath, where the family lived. Here he met and worked with John Arthur Roebuck Rudge, an instrument maker and inventor, who had adapted a magic lantern to create the illusion of movement by showing seven slides in quick succession. This inspired Friese-Greene to develop better machines: he sold the studios and moved to London, where he believed there were better prospects.

In 1885 he was lodging with his cousin Alfred Carter at 26 Aldershot Road on the Willesden side of Kilburn, off Willesden Lane. That year he met two brothers, Esme and Arthur Collings, and they went into partnership. He put up £200 and they started at 69 Bond Street, in two rooms above a shoe shop. They were very successful, and in 1887 opened another photographic studio at 92 Piccadilly, facing Green Park, with a workshop behind the underground studio.

In 1888 Friese-Greene rented No.136 Maida Vale and brought his wife and daughter Ethel to live there. In addition to Bond Street and Piccadilly he had two studios near Whiteley's, with Arthur Collings in charge. At the time, he thought he was making more than a thousand pounds a year, although he did not really know, as he had no time for keeping accounts.

The Maida Vale house (see p 28) had a large basement which he used as a workroom. The chemicals he used had a smell which Helena hated, so he took his 'stink lab' to a small laboratory in Brooke Street, Holborn. The critical moment is described in his biography:

By 1889 Friese-Greene had developed a camera which took moving pictures. He invited Alf Carter and his 3-year-old son Bert to meet him at Hyde Park on a Sunday morning, and set up his camera and tripod near Apsley House. First he exposed 20 feet of film showing Alf and Bert playing, and then moved across the road to shoot the rest of the 50 feet of celluloid film, showing pedestrians, buses and cabs. William went back to Kilburn for the afternoon before going to his Holborn laboratory to develop and view the film. He was so excited at what he saw that he rushed into the street shouting 'I've got it! I've got it!' He dragged a passing policeman into the lab to show him the film of the 'Sunday Parade', then walked home to Maida Vale and drank champagne with Helena to celebrate.

It is claimed Friese-Greene showed his first film at the Royal Photographic convention in Chester Town Hall in July 1890. However, some film historians dispute this, arguing that projection would not have been possible with the equipment existing at the time. A few months later Eastman's celluloid film became available in this country and Friese-Green immediately began using it. Working with Frederick Varley, he improved the camera designs, demonstrating them at photographic societies, and at the same time, experimented with various means of projection. Using up the considerable profits from his photographic studios for his development work, he was sued for debt and imprisoned for a short period in 1891. The following year he was declared bankrupt. However, he managed to make some money from his patents for high-speed printing of photographs. Debts forced the family to leave Maida Vale in February 1891 and they moved to 39 King's Road, Chelsea where they opened a new studio.

By 1895 commercial moving pictures were beginning to be shown in Europe led by Edison, the Lumières and Robert Paul. Friese-Greene's contribution was largely forgotten. His wife had been in poor health for some time and she died in 1895. In 1897 he married Edith Harrison and they had six sons. From the late 1890s on, Friese-Greene concentrated on producing moving pictures in colour, and by 1905 he had a working system, using alternating colour filters. At this time the family were living in Brighton, but his experiments proved expensive and by 1910 he was bankrupt again. At the beginning of WW I the family were so poor that a friend organised a collection for them from the film industry. It all became too much for his wife, who left William in 1917. During the War he worked for the Government and afterwards returned to his colour experiments, registering a total of 78 patents between 1889 and 1921.

On 5 May 1921 Friese-Greene attended a major meeting of film distributors at the Connaught Rooms in Great Queen Street. He stood up to make a speech in which he wondered what a film of his life might be like and whether it would tell the truth. He spoke incoherently and there were shouts from the audience to 'Speak up'. He was helped back to his seat, then, bent forward with his head in his hands, he died. His pocket contained just one shilling and tenpence, apparently all the money he possessed. The film industry gave Friese-Greene an impressive funeral on 13 May 1921 and commissioned a monument designed by Sir Edwin Lutyens for his grave in Highgate cemetery. The tombstone is inscribed 'the inventor of Kinematography' with his patent number 10,131. All the cinemas in Britain halted their showings for a 2-minute silence during his funeral. In 1951 for the Festival of Britain, John Boulting directed the film *The Magic Box*, based on Allister's biography, as a tribute to Friese-Greene. He is played by Robert Donat and the policeman by Laurence Olivier, while his cousin is played by Dickie Attenborough.

No.138 Maida Vale, previously variously numbered Nos.8, 9 and 10 Kilburn Priory

William Cullum, china and glass manufacturer, d. 1895

This was one of the largest plots on the estate and the house was commensurately grand, built soon after 1840. William Cullum was probably the first occupant of the house. Cullum was a property speculator as well as a manufacturer. His father was a china dealer in Judd Street and when he took over, William greatly expanded the business, going into partnership with the Sharpus Brothers. They opened 'Sharpus and Cullum' in Cockspur Street and the firm exhibited at the 1851 Great Exhibition. Cullum gave one of his sons the middle name of 'Sharpus'. Cullum speculated on the Upton estate, where he owned the five properties adjacent to his own. Ultimately he preferred a more 'rural' style of living, and in 1852 he bought 6 acres of farmland across the Edgware Road in Willesden where he built 'Malvern House', moving his family there in 1856. The house still stands in Malvern Road, currently used as offices. Cullum died there, aged 95, in 1895.

No.138 Maida Vale was demolished and the site was used first for a fire station and then a telephone exchange.

No.140 Maida Vale, previously No.9 Kilburn Priory, also known as South Lodge.

This was one of the first houses completed on the estate in 1823 and appears on some maps as 'Priory Cottage'. This was a conceit – the house was another splendid mansion, as witnessed by the sale details below, by which time it had a more appropriate name. Despite duplication of the house number, this property seems to have been consistently described as No.9 Kilburn Priory or South Lodge, before being included under Maida Vale.

Benjamin Shaw was the second occupant, moving in two years after the house was completed. A wealthy man, Shaw made an unsuccessful offer for George Pocock's house (the original No.7) at a time when Pocock was trying to sell off his assets and clear his debts. Shaw died in January 1861, aged 94, at which time he had only recently left Kilburn Priory. In April his old house came up for sale and was advertised as:

> South Lodge: Excellent detached villa, pleasant healthy position, 8 bedrooms, dressing room, 4 reception rooms, music room, leading to a vinery and a conservatory. Stabling, coach house, long lease.

Major General John Theophilus Boileau, army officer, 1805–1886

The retired Major General Boileau rented 'South Lodge' in the late 1850s. The 1861 census shows his large household: Eleven members of his family plus three servants. Aged 58, Boileau was born in Calcutta and served in the Bengal Engineers. He married Ann Hanson in 1829 and they had twelve children. Boileau was responsible for many building projects in India: churches, jails, bridges, barracks and public works of every description. He returned to England in 1857, and moved to Kilburn where he had links with a local volunteer company, the Victoria Rifles. Their rifle ground was in open fields near the corner of the present Kilburn High Road and Victoria Road. The Duke of Wellington offered Boileau the command of the Rifles, but the General preferred to join the ranks as a private. In 1860, Boileau accompanied the Duke and other notables to a shooting competition at the company grounds in Kilburn.

Boileau died in 1886 and his obituary noted he was 'equally eminent as an engineer, scientist, man of business and philanthropist'. Sadly, owing to 'losses in the Agra Bank and elsewhere', Boileau's daughters were left poorly provided for, and a fund was opened for them under the auspices of Boileau's old friend, Field Marshall Lord Napier of Magdala.

Henry Sweet, phonetician and philologist, 1845–1912

The Sweet family followed Boileau at South Lodge and were there from at least 1864 to 1879. George Sweet was a barrister whose speciality was conveyancing, and he wrote a series of books on the subject. Henry was the eldest of his three sons. From childhood Henry was interested in alphabets and languages, and he decided on a career in philology.

Shortly after his father's death in 1879, Henry moved to Hampstead, into lodgings on Heath Street. In November he wrote 'the air was very fine' and he 'could get out into a very fine country in a few minutes.' His friends wrote that he lived a hermit-like existence until his marriage in 1887. He wrote some of his most important works here including the *Epinal Glossary*, and he started the *New English Grammar*.

Sweet supported himself and his wife by means of a legacy plus income from his publications and by taking in pupils who required language tuition. In 1894 the couple moved to Oxford, where Sweet was eventually appointed to the newly established post of Reader in Phonetics. Bernard Shaw called Sweet 'the greatest English phonetician of his time' and it is said that he was the model for Shaw's character Professor Higgins in 'Pygmalion'.

140 Maida Vale was demolished to make way for the Maida Vale Picture Palace, which opened in 1913.

Nos.2-8 (even) Kilburn Priory, previously Nos.10-13 consec Kilburn Priory were built between 1841 and 1847.

No.4 Kilburn Priory, previously No.11 Kilburn Priory

John George Swindell, d. 1850
See p 34.

Louisa Elizabeth Harris
On 10 February 1912, Mrs Louisa Elizabeth Harris died at 4 Kilburn Priory. She left specific orders in her will:

> *I most sincerely desire that there shall be no possibility of my being buried alive or put under the ground alive or in a trance, and there shall be the most undoubted proof of death by one or more fully qualified medical men after personally seeing my body. I have none at present in whom I have sufficient confidence to name, so must leave to my executors to choose those who are perfectly capable of judging that decomposition has really set in before being fastened down and buried.*

There is no record of whether the will was read in time to carry out her instruction.

No.6 Kilburn Priory, previously No.12 Kilburn Priory

In 1862, **James Cooke** of 12 Kilburn Priory placed an advert in *The Times*:
'Lost, warrant, for one hogshead of brandy, ex Ironmaster, Captain Parkman, from Charente. Whoever finds the above shall be rewarded.'

No.8 Kilburn Priory, previously No.13 Kilburn Priory

Michael Coomes, bookseller
Coomes, a successful bookseller, moved into the Kilburn Priory house in the mid-1850s and stayed for nearly 30 years. Coomes ran a bookshop and lending library at 141 Regent Street. In the 1860s, he charged a basic yearly subscription of one guinea for town customers to borrow books and three guineas for country subscribers, who could borrow sixteen books at a time: 'a larger number than is allowed by any other library. .. All the best new works are added on the day of publication'. A business continued trading at this address using the Coomes name until the early 1890s.

No.10 Kilburn Priory, previously No.14 Kilburn Priory. Also known as Kilburn Lodge, or Kilburn Grove

This was another early-built house, dating from about 1823 and standing alone for many years by the side of the 'Private Road'. The second occupant was William Radford. In 1828, young John Pocock notes in his diary that his uncle John had 'taken' Radford's property, 'intending to keep a country house'. Radford's house has been identified incorrectly as 18 Greville Place.

Nos.14 -20 (even) Kilburn Priory, previously Nos.16-19 sequential Kilburn Priory (numbers changed about 1885)

The 1861 census notes these four houses as 'building'.

No.14 Kilburn Priory, previously No.16 Kilburn Priory

Sir James William Redhouse, lexicographer, 1811–1892

Redhouse was probably the first occupant of the house and he stayed there until his death in 1892. At the age of 15 James was expelled from Christ's Hospital School because of truancy and he had no further formal education. He became a cabin boy on a merchantman and travelled to the Mediterranean. He slipped ship in Constantinople and by 1828 had become a teacher in the Ottoman naval academy. He remained, on and off, in the Ottoman service until 1853, and travelled widely for his work. Redhouse obviously had an aptitude for languages and learned Turkish, Persian, Arabic, French, Italian and several other languages within a few years of arriving in Constantinople. He produced several linguistic publications, including a book of Ottoman definitions of widely used Arabic and Persian words, which was used for many years in schools. On the eve of the Crimean War health problems forced Redhouse to return to England, where he worked as oriental translator at the Foreign Office. He also published further books including a *Turkish and English Lexicon* which became the standard work and is still used today by at least one American missionary organisation. He was awarded a knighthood for his diplomatic work in 1888. Redhouse died at Kilburn in 1892 and was buried in Brookwood Cemetery: a humble cabin boy who had risen to a knighthood!

No.16 Kilburn Priory, previously No.17 Kilburn Priory

Thomas Smith Café, artist, d. 1869

Thomas Smith Café may have moved here from Newman Street. He was probably the first occupant of this house, but he died at Kilburn Priory only a few years later in 1869. The house was put up for rent soon after, and his collection of art works was auctioned in 1870. The house was described as a 'Charming bijou villa, Maida Hill, drawing, dining and breakfast rooms, conservatory, four bedrooms, coach house, stable, grapery, ¼ acre garden, croquet lawn.'

No.20 Kilburn Priory, previously No.19 Kilburn Priory

In September 1868, Eliza Wiggins was charged with stealing from her mistress, Mrs Sylvia Brockell of 19 Kilburn Priory, a shawl, three petticoats and other items to a value of £7. When her room was searched, a quantity of Mrs Brockell's property was found, including a missing bunch of keys 'which would open almost every drawer in the house'. Eliza's former employer had given her a good reference, and although she was found guilty, the jury recommended that mercy be shown, and Mrs Brockell agreed. Eliza was sentenced to 6 months, with hard labour.

(here is Greville Road)

WEST SIDE (see map on p 42)

No.3 Kilburn Priory

John Pitt-Hardacre, theatrical manager, d. 1933

A street directory of 1926 shows Pitt-Hardacre at this address. He turns out to have an interesting history and was continually in and out of court protecting his rights to the popular play *East Lynne*.

Hardacre began his theatrical life in Manchester in 1876 on a salary of just 3 shillings a week. After some time this was increased to 9 shillings, due to his talent for playing 14 or 15 different characters in the same evening. Hardacre

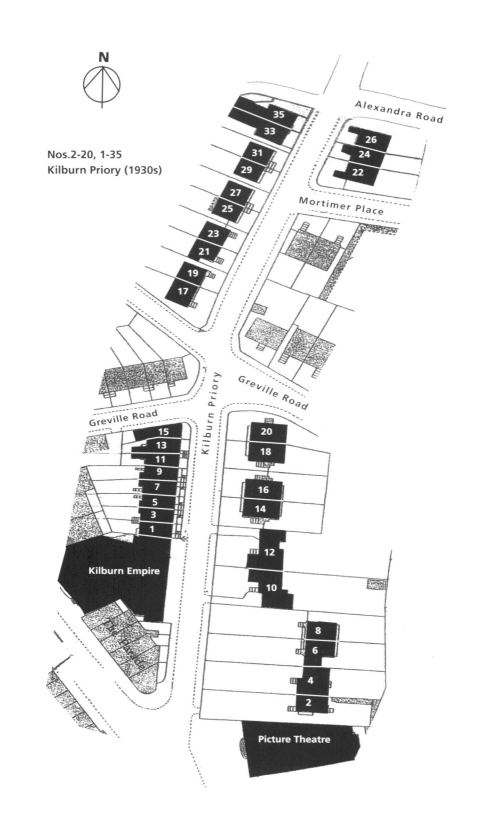

N

Nos.2-20, 1-35
Kilburn Priory (1930s)

Alexandra Road

35
33
31
29
27
25
23
21
19
17

26
24
22

Mortimer Place

Kilburn Priory

Greville Road

Greville Road

15
13
11
9
7
5
3
1

Kilburn Empire

20
18

16
14

12

10

8
6

4

2

Picture Theatre

progressed to management and bought several theatres, settling at the Comedy, one of the newest theatres in Manchester, in 1890. He also became a member of the Town Council.

East Lynne, a novel written by Mrs Henry Wood, was dramatised by John Coleman Chute, who later added the role of a comic policeman to the play. The popular actor Wilson Barratt and his brother George toured the play with great success. In 1888 Hardacre paid Chute £12 for the performing rights of this version. In one of the trials in 1904, Hardacre said the play had been performed 6,000 times since 1888. He had taken action against other people for playing *East Lynne*, and in all cases they either withdrew or paid his costs of the proceedings.

There were other less savoury court appearances. In 1902 Edward Holt, a member of the Watch committee in Manchester, brought a case against Hardacre. He was accused of having intercourse with several women in his private room in the theatre, and four girls made accusations against him. Hardacre lost the case, the action cost him the amazing sum of £30,000 and his marriage collapsed. He sold the theatre a year later. Then at a meeting in 1905, Councillor Williams said that among musicians the Comedy theatre was known as 'The Harem', that there were instances which would shame a French brothel. When Hardacre sued Williams he won, and received £50 damages. Hardacre lived long enough to see a film version of *East Lynne* made in 1931, starring Clive Brook. He died in a London nursing home.

(here is Springfield Lane)

No.27 Kilburn Priory, previously No.14 Springfield Villas

Variously reported as occurring on the evening of Christmas Eve or Christmas Day 1890, a massive gas explosion ripped through Miss Maria Goldby's house in Kilburn Priory. She was away at the time. Mrs McBain, the caretaker, had smelled gas and called a workman. James Protheroe turned off the gas and told the caretaker not to light any lamps. He went to fetch his tools and on his return, the door was opened by Mrs McBain, carrying a light. The resultant explosion wrecked most of the house: poor Protheroe was hurled against the area wall and badly hurt, but the caretaker escaped injury. Large crowds came to view the damaged house.

No.33 Kilburn Priory, previously No.17 Springfield Villas

George C. Maund, artist, d. 1871
Shown at this address in the early 1860s, his speciality was landscapes. His 1871 RA exhibit was entitled 'Hampstead Priory'. Maund died shortly afterwards.

Hamilton P. McCarthy, sculptor
McCarthy was living here by 1878, probably moving here from Charlotte Street. Although recorded in the 1881 census he had left Kilburn by 1882, when he exhibited from Mortimer Street. He was a specialist in portrait busts.

No.35 Kilburn Priory, previously No.18 Springfield Villas

In 1885, an inquest was held on Henry Philip Stride of 35 Kilburn Priory. His body was found in the tunnel of the Metropolitan line, between St John's Wood and Baker Street stations. Stride had worked as a press reader for a publisher near Fleet Street. A porter at Baker Street gave evidence. He was shutting the doors of the third-class carriages on the 7.29 train to Pinner, and had to run down the platform, trying to close a door that was blocked by a passenger's coat. Another passenger followed him and cannoned into him, knocking him off the platform into some barrows. When he got up the man was gone; he therefore concluded that the passenger had succeeded in getting into the train. Perhaps this was Stride, but no one could be certain; the verdict recorded that Stride had died from injuries received on the line 'but there was no direct evidence to show how he came there'.

MAIDA VALE

No.138 Maida Vale: Kilburn Fire Station and Maida Vale telephone exchange

In 1898, the LCC was looking for a suitable site for a Kilburn fire substation. The Committee decided that with adaptation, 138 Maida Vale could be suitable and the legal machinery was set in motion to acquire the house and grounds. Negotiations between the LCC and the freeholder, Capt. J F Bagot, dragged on for 4 years. Bagot refused to accept the Council's offer for the site, and it was finally decided that a formal sealed offer should be made for the property. At the same time, the LCC noted that William Sharpus Cullum had a leasehold interest in the house. In March 1902 Bagot informed the authorities he would take £980 for the property, which was slightly more than the sealed offer. Hampstead Council later noted that a 'wood and iron fire station building' was to be built on part of the forecourt, but this was a temporary structure; a 'street station' in the garden was established by 1903.

[11] Kilburn Fire Station on site of former 138 Maida Vale

In July 1903 the LCC's plans were complete, and building work began in November. The memorial stone was laid on 25 February 1904 (as reported in the *Kilburn Times*). Edward Smith, Chairman of the LCC Fire Brigade Committee officiated, returning in November to open the building **[11]**. He explained the growth of the Fire Service in response to changing circumstances: '*Years ago, neighbourhoods were covered with market-gardens, they were now covered by houses and babies.*' The station was equipped with the most modern appliances at a total cost of £9,601, Mr Smith concluded that if '*any fault was to be found with the station it was that it was rather too good!*' An alarm was given by a wife of one of the councillors attending the ceremony, and the brigade emerged into Maida Vale to loud cheers from the crowd.

Surprisingly, the station functioned for less than 20 years. The Post Office bought the building in 1922 and converted it into the Maida Vale telephone exchange **[12]** on 9 September. '*The new exchange .. is of the modern central battery type with lamp indicator signals*'. In 2006 the exchange is still operational.

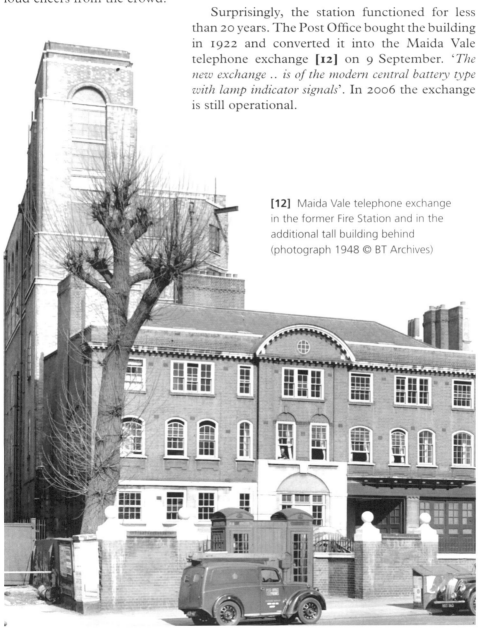

[12] Maida Vale telephone exchange in the former Fire Station and in the additional tall building behind (photograph 1948 © BT Archives)

No.140 Maida Vale: Maida Vale Picture Palace

In 1911 the first plans for a cinema on this site were agreed by the LCC but the project did not go ahead. A second plan was subsequently approved, the local press reported the site cleared in August 1912, and the Maida Vale Picture Palace opened [13] on 27 January 1913. Edward Stone designed the building, he was also the architect for the Grange Cinema on Kilburn High Road and the London Astoria. A seven-piece orchestra conducted by Mr Paiba accompanied the silent films. When Paiba was replaced by Signor de Perugia, gold medallist of the Florence Conservatoire, the local paper reported a significant improvement. In 1927 a Grand Wurlitzer organ was installed, so powerful that neighbours in Greville Place complained about the noise and tried unsuccessfully to block renewal of the cinema's licence. In 1929 'sound' was installed by the new owners Gaumont, and 'talkies' were shown for the first time.

[13] Advertisement for the Maida Vale Palace (February 1913)

With seating for 1500, this 'palatial building' was seen as London's most luxurious picture theatre, with its two imposing towers and coppered domes [14]. The foyer had a marbled floor, the walls were panelled in oak and the colour scheme was royal blue and gold. Admission prices started at 6d rising to 2/-, and a curtained box cost between 7/6 and 10/6. Before the show, patrons could wait either in the lounge or the tearoom. The last films were shown in 1940 and a restaurant opened there the following year. In 1949 it became the 'Carlton Rooms', a social club and entertainment venue featuring dance bands such as Victor Sylvester. When the Mecca Social Club opened in 1961 it was reported to be the first commercial Bingo hall in the country, and it continued up until 1996. The exterior of this Grade II Listed building is remarkably well preserved and it is currently used by the 'Islamic Centre England – London', which opened in 1998.

Kilburn Gate estate

See p 27 for Hampstead Council's Kilburn Gate scheme (1946).

Murray Melvin, actor

Melvin is shown to be living here in a 1962 directory. Murray Melvin appeared in over 50 films, including *A Taste of Honey* in 1962. He worked regularly with Ken Russell, in *Isadora Duncan*, *The Devils*, *The Boyfriend*, *Lisztomania*, *Clouds of Glory* and *Prisoners of Honour*. He also made numerous TV appearances. Today he is the archivist of the Theatre Royal, Stratford where he worked for many years with Joan Littlewood. He remembers his early days:

> *In 1957, I had a £2 a week grant and a place at the Guildhall Drama School, but instead of going to college I walked in off the street and offered my services to Joan and Gerry (Joan Littlewood's partner Gerry Raffles, the General Manager) who had come to Stratford with their Theatre Workshop in 1953. The theatre was terribly hard up, so like everyone in the company I mucked in. I painted the foyer, built sets, sewed on buttons, cleared the drains and appeared in the plays that Joan Littlewood directed – a new one every fortnight – here at the Theatre Royal. I'm a North London boy, and in those days it took hours to get home to Hampstead on the train, so I often used to sleep in the theatre. My first major role, in 1958, was in Shelagh Delaney's 'A Taste of Honey', and in the same year I played the Tommy soldier in Brendan Behan's 'The Hostage'. This production was my favourite, partly because by that time I was a little more secure as a performer. In the bar, Brendan's laughter and stories held us enthralled for hours, and it was one huge party. And the play was such fun, though of course, it was very hard work – that didn't change. Then, in 1963, I was in the original cast of 'Oh What a Lovely War'.*

[14] The former Maida Vale Picture Palace in 2006

6 Greville Place and Greville Road

GREVILLE PLACE (see map on p 49)

Pocock drove this road, sometimes referred to as Greville Hill, across the open fields. The name was chosen in recognition of the landowner. Originally, the numbering was sequential, up the east side from the Edgware Road and down the west side. This was established by 1830. It was renumbered around 1862, when the east frontage was given even numbers and the west side odd ones.

WEST SIDE, from Maida Vale

Nos.1-11 odd Greville Place, previously Nos.14-8 consec Nos.13-19 odd Greville Place

There is further confusion over numbering so far as Nos.1 and 3 (originally three houses) are concerned. They were numbered 5, 4 and 3 until 1830, when they were renumbered as 14, 13 and 12.

Between 1822 and 1827, Nos.4 and 3 were separately occupied. In 1828 a school took over both properties, and while the Rates continued to allocate two numbers, the houses are shown as jointly occupied. However, the Census took the view that as Nos.12 and 13 were occupied as one, the single number '12' would suffice to describe them. Thus the house next door was generally called No.13, not 14!

There were also two properties numbered 1a at different times, both now demolished.

No.1a Greville Place, The Croft

A plot of open ground separated the rear garden walls of houses on the main road, later Nos.128-136 Maida Vale, and the side wall of No.1 Greville Place. This land may once have formed part of George Pocock's *large and luxurious garden full of choice fruit trees and vegetables* behind his own Kilburn Priory mansion. There was apparently a stable or coach house on the land, but by 1891 this had been replaced by a house, No.1a Greville Place, also called 'The Croft'. Subsequent building extensions created a low, linear property that spread along much of the boundary wall with the Maida Vale houses. The Croft and the adjacent houses Nos.128-134 Maida Vale were demolished and their site was used for a block of flats, Vivian Court.

Bertrand Phillips

In 1909 Phillips, then living in Kent, was declared bankrupt. In 1904 his family had helped pay the debts he had run up, but since then, Phillips had incurred substantial losses by gambling on the Stock Exchange and betting. He was living in 'The Croft' by 1921, and stayed until 1930, when the house was advertised for sale: *'planned on the lines of a country cottage'*, with the main accommodation chiefly on one floor. Phillips held a separate auction to dispose of the contents, including items of antique furniture and art works. In 1938, Phillips, who was then living in Maida Vale, was in the bankruptcy court again. Payments to support his family under a Trust were cited, as well as gambling debts. The court was told that in 1935 Phillips had lost nearly £6,000 in just three days at Ascot Races.

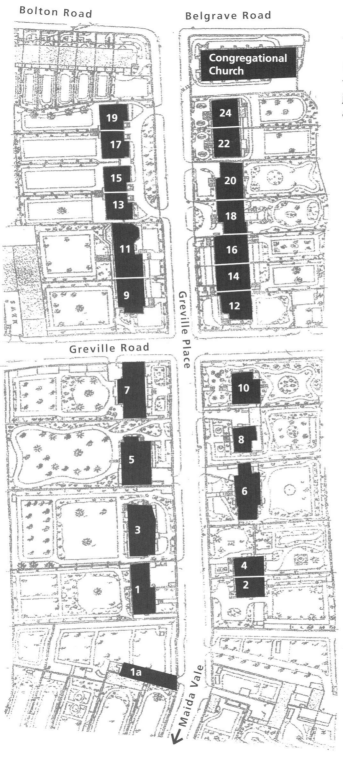

Bolton Road

Belgrave Road

Congregational Church

Nos.1-24 Greville Place,
from Maida Vale to
junction with Belgrave
and Bolton Roads (1868)

19

17

15

13

11

9

24

22

20

18

16

14

12

Greville Place

Greville Road

7

5

3

1

10

8

6

4

2

1a

Maida Vale

No.1 Greville Place, previously No.14 (or 13) Greville Place. Grade II listed
John Murray, 5th Duke of Atholl, 1778–1846 and
Captain James Murray, recruiting officer for the East India Company

Captain Murray of the East India Company arrived in Kilburn in 1826 and stayed until the late 1830s, when he probably moved to the company office at 28 Soho Square. James Murray was a friend of George Pocock, whose eldest son George Felix was a gunner in the East India Company. There are several references in Pocock's younger son's diary to visiting Captain Murray at his office in Soho Square to deliver letters to be forwarded to Felix, and on one sad occasion to notify him of his father's death. This link probably explains how Murray came to be renting in Kilburn, but not why – perhaps because from 1826 to 1830, Captain Murray was also the paid 'keeper' of John Murray, Duke of Atholl, and No.1 was a detached and fairly isolated house [15]. We do not know if the Murrays were related.

Born in 1778, John Murray was the son of the 4th Duke of Atholl. John, with the courtesy title Lord Tullibardine, was a good-looking, bright young man. But he soon showed signs of what today we would call a bipolar disorder: appearing highly excitable one moment and deeply reflective the next. At the age of 20 he was sent to Portugal with his regiment, accompanied by his personal physician, Dr Alexander Menzies. When they arrived John began to show alarming symptoms which could no longer be dismissed as mere mood swings. The family always believed John had

[15] No.1 Greville Place in 2005

been struck on the head, while Menzies thought it was the result of heat stroke. Whatever the cause, on the 13 April 1798 Menzies felt obliged to write in strictest confidence to the family physician, Sir Walter Farquhar: *'I think it my duty to inform you that on Friday last, I discovered some appearances of mental derangement'*. As there was a history of mental instability in the family, Menzies was understandably reluctant to tell the Duke that his son was mad, and asked Farquhar to pass on the bad news. Meanwhile, Menzies undertook to keep the matter as secret as possible, but *'the attack was so violent and unexpected that in the circumstances in which he was placed, in a garrison under military command, it was impossible to conceal it'*. He arranged to bring John back to England as soon as possible.

Back in London, Menzies again wrote to Farquhar on 22 June 1798:

He seems lost in thought and speaks to himself. He is subject to incoherency and false judgements and is even at times violent. One day he was allowed to walk out, but he was so desirous of making his escape that he applied to persons whom he met to rescue him. About eight days ago he fairly got over the garden wall and over the wall of another small enclosure, tho' pursued by the servant who got hold of him in the fields. He is at times so absent that he seems ill pleased at having the train of his thoughts interrupted by a question. One day recently he was convinced that he was then confined and punished for a mutiny he had been guilty of in Lisbon, and two days afterwards he wished to work for his bread and blamed the Duke of Atholl for allowing his son to be reduced to these circumstances. The work he wished for was to dig with a spade. When opposed in anything he eagerly wishes, he will not hesitate to strike any person.….About ten days ago the person who attends him gave him a knife to eat his dinner, which I had seldom ventured to do. He started up from the table suddenly with the knife in his hand, and attacked the man, who was obliged to defend himself with a chair.

Sadly, John never recovered his senses. At first he lived in Hoxton with a Mr Warburton and then with Captain James Murray and his wife at Kilburn. Family records indicate that Murray was 'dismissed' in 1830, but no reason is given. The death of John's father the 4th Duke of Atholl delayed the appointment of Captain Murray's replacement, and there is no record of what happened next. Bearing in mind the Duke was still living in No.1 Greville Place in 1841, it seems likely Captain Murray continued in post until he left Greville Place, when his place was taken by Patrick Macintyre (see later), who looked after the Duke until he died.

As head of the East India Company's recruiting service, Captain Murray was involved in a bizarre case in 1831, concerning a young girl called Louisa Sale. Louisa claimed to be a native of St Helena, where her father was a Captain of Grenadiers in the East India Company. She said she had been abducted by a couple called Goodison, who had taken her on board a ship which had then sailed for England. Put to work selling matches door-to-door, Louisa was befriended by a Mrs Crew, who sought advice from a magistrate, 'as it was a dreadful thing if the child's statement was true, that her parents should be left in utter ignorance of her fate'. When Captain Murray confirmed there was a Captain Sale in the Company's service in St Helena, the magistrate ordered that Louisa be returned to her parents.

Captain Murray was called to give evidence on at least two more occasions. One concerned a fraudulent attempt to obtain a discharge from the East India Company and the other concerned a man who had taken money from five different Company sergeants under the pretence of enlisting with each. On being arrested, he had seriously assaulted a police constable. He was sent for trial as *'it was not Captain Murray's wish to receive a person with such a character into the corps'*.

Patrick Macintyre and Phoebe Macintyre, painter (c.1790–1863)

The 1841 census shows Patrick Macintyre as the main householder at 1 Greville Place, living with his wife Phoebe. But the house was also still home to His Grace the Duke of Atholl, aged 60, plus two male and two female servants.

The Duke occupied a padded room, where there were no windows for him to break. The small household kept him out of harm's way, while family affairs were run by his younger brother, Lord Glenlyon. Aged 68, the Duke died almost unnoticed at Kilburn on 14 September 1846. The cause of death is given as 'Ascites from chronic peritonitis. Certified two years' (ascites is an abnormal accumulation of fluid in the abdominal cavity). Patrick Macintyre was the witness on the death certificate. *The Times* carried only a single paragraph about the Duke's death on 19 September 1846:

> *In recording the decease of the fifth Duke of Atholl, there is little more to be stated than the fact that for many years past he lived in perfect seclusion at a suburban villa near St John's wood. His mental condition excluded him from intercourse with general society, and from the management of his affairs. He was succeeded by his nephew.*

On the face of it Patrick Macintyre does not appear to be a natural choice as guardian of the Duke. The census gives his profession as Secretary of the United Kingdom Assurance Company, with offices off Pall Mall. Perhaps his wife was the main carer. Macintyre had married Phoebe Dighton, artist and widow of the painter Denis Dighton. In 1830 she was appointed 'fruit and flower painter' to Queen Adelaide and between 1841 and 1854 sent three paintings from 13 Greville Place to the Royal Academy annual show.

Although they retained the house in Greville Place, the couple left Kilburn after the Duke's death. They travelled abroad and produced a handwritten account in two volumes of their experiences in Switzerland during 1848 and 1849, illustrated by Phoebe's drawings (this appeared in the catalogue of a dealer in rare books in Fribourg). The books contain advice to travellers concerning what to pack: 'telescope, opera-glass, medicine, a box of Lucifers, a knife and (last but not least!) a flask of brandy'. The couple visited Basle, Zurich, Gruyères and Geneva and ascended the St Bernard Pass. The illustrations include one of 'Barry', the most famous of the St Bernard rescue dogs.

In 1851 the Macintyres were at Kensington Gate, but they returned to Kilburn where they were still living when Phoebe died in Edinburgh 'from fatigue' while looking after her sick husband.

Thomas James Arnold, barrister and literary translator, 1803–1877

Thomas James Arnold was born in Downing Street, Westminster, the eldest son of the dramatist Samuel Arnold who wrote the song *The Death of Nelson* containing the famous line *'Our ships were British oak, And hearts of oak our men'*. Thomas was a lawyer on the northern circuit, and then a magistrate in London; when he died at 1 Greville Place on 20 May 1877 he was the senior London police magistrate. *The Times* observed: *'it was never known that any of his decisions which had been appealed against were reversed by the Superior Courts'*. Arnold wrote legal manuals but was also known for his translations of Goethe, Ovid, Euripides and Aristophanes. He was buried in Kensal Green Cemetery.

Sir John Primatt Maud KCB CBE, Baron Redcliffe-Maud, civil servant, 1906–1982

John Maud is shown in directories at 1 Greville Place from at least 1951 to 1965. He was appointed master of Birkbeck College, London University in 1939 and held this post throughout the war while also working as a civil servant in the Ministry of Food. He was appointed Permanent Secretary at the Ministry of Education in 1945, and was one of the founders of UNESCO. In 1952 he became Permanent Secretary to the Ministry of Fuel and Power. In 1959 Harold Wilson sent him to South Africa as the British High Commissioner. By 1963 he returned as Master of University College Oxford, a post he held until his retirement in 1976. During this time he chaired a succession of public inquiries. He was a skilled public speaker. His wife Jean Hamilton was a professional concert pianist. Sir John died in Oxford in 1982.

No.1a Greville Place, originally part of No.1, demolished

Among the last occupants of this property, which was probably originally a coach house, were believed to be members of the 'Pink Floyd' rock group, but in answer to our enquiry one of the band has written saying that none of them ever lived there. Demolished in the 1970s, the site of this house and garden now forms the 'Greville Place Nature Reserve', established in 1985 by Camden Council and open to the public once a month by appointment.

No.3 Greville Place, previously Nos.12 and 13 Greville Place. Grade II listed. Also known as Greville House

The rear of the house has been extended into the garden and the house has been subdivided to provide a number of separate dwellings.

George Henry Gibbons

In 1822, George Henry Gibbons was the first occupant of this house. Six years later, in March 1828 he was charged, along with seven others, with attempting to defraud the East India Company by unlawfully selling a cadetship. At his court appearance in June, one of the accused spoke up for Gibbons, saying that his wife was dangerously ill, and that '*if the sentence of the Court should doom (Gibbons) to gaol, he might probably never see her again*'. Gibbons was allowed home on condition that he return at a later date for sentencing. In November he received three months' imprisonment.

The Misses Giblett's Academy/School/Seminary

The school moved here from No.4 Kilburn Priory in 1828, presumably after the Gibbons court case, and remained for over 40 years. The Giblett surname appears in various spellings. Several Miss Gibletts are recorded as teachers: Sophia and Frances (Kilburn Priory) and later Eliza, Mary and Fanny. From 15 girls shown in the 1841 census, the number of pupils dropped to only four residents by 1861. The 'Seminary' is still listed in the 1869 Post Office Directory, but had closed by the time of the 1871 census, presumably because of the declining numbers.

Henry Saxon Snell, FRIBA, architect, 1832–1904.

Snell took on the property after the Gibletts' school closed. He was an architect who mainly designed hospitals and Poor Law institutions. During his career, which spanned 40 years, he acted as architect to 27 metropolitan and suburban parishes. His son Alfred was also an architect and worked with his father. Locally, the firm built a workhouse infirmary that became the Archway Wing of the Whittington Hospital, Highgate.

In August 1870 Snell advertised for builders to tender for alterations and repairs to the house. He obtained seven quotes, ranging from £716 to £593. The work was presumably complete by the time of the 1871 census, which records him living in the property with his family, including ten children. 'Greville House', 3 Greville Place, was advertised for sale or to let in 1879, when the lease was valued at £1,500. The property was described as standing in nearly half an acre of ground, with a *large croquet lawn, skating rink 100 foot long, fully stocked kitchen and fruit garden*'. There were 11 bedrooms and 6 reception rooms. It had been '*lately remodelled, redrained and decorated by an architect*'. The skating rink (perhaps for roller skating, which was popular at the time), may have been left over from the time the house was a school, and the architect referred to must have been Snell. In 1877 his son Harry married Annie Maria Potter, the daughter of Thomas Potter who lived at Poplar House, West End, and owned an iron foundry there (see 128 Maida Vale, p 35).

Harris John Holland, gunmaker, 1806–1896

Holland was living at 3 Greville Place at the time of the 1881 and 1891 censuses and he stayed until his death in 1896. Harris Holland initially ran a wholesale tobacco business. He was an entrepreneur with a keen interest in pigeon shooting and he began to make and sell guns in 1835. His nephew Henry Holland joined the business in 1861, and the partnership of Holland and Holland was created in 1876. This famous gun company is still in business today and their high-quality rifles and sporting guns command high prices. Holland was buried at Kensal Green Cemetery.

Sir Francis (Frank) Dicksee, RA, artist, 1853–1928

Frank Dicksee lived at 3 Greville Place for many years, from about 1898 to 1926. He was the eldest son of the painter and illustrator Thomas Dicksee. He studied art at the Royal Academy Schools and won medals early in his career. His style was firmly Pre-Raphaelite and he was greatly influenced by Burne-Jones and William Morris. Dicksee was a vehement opponent of modern art. His romantic work was popular and sold well during his lifetime. He was elected president of the Royal Academy in 1924 and was knighted the following year. His sister **Margaret Dicksee**, also an artist, lived with him. He died unmarried on 17 October 1928 at the Cambridge Nursing Home in Dorset Square, London. The house was home to other artists after Dicksee's death. The studio was up for sale in 1994, priced £425,000.

Madame Lydia Kyasht, ballerina, 1885–1959

After the Dicksees left, Madame Lydia Kyasht, the Russian ballerina [16], opened a dance school at 3a Greville Place in 1934. She was there till 1936 and then moved her Academy of Dance to 10a Kilburn High Road, where it lasted until 1940. Born in St Petersburg in 1885, she trained at the Imperial Ballet School where Pavlova was a fellow student. In 1902 Lydia joined the Mariinsky Theatre and became the premier dancer. She later claimed that she, and not Pavlova, first performed the Dying Swan in 1905. Lydia came to London in 1908 as prima ballerina at the Empire Theatre Leicester Square, where she worked until 1913. Her first role was in *Coppélia*: a newspaper review said, 'she was as pretty as a china doll...but we were appalled by her very short tutu'. In her autobiography, Lady Diana Cooper wrote '*I went to Lydia Kyasht to be taught to glide like a Russian peasant, flicking a provocative red handkerchief. A year's work taught me to stop learning*'.

Lydia danced in Diaghilev's Ballets Russes in 1912 and 1919, and lived in Russia for about 5 years. In 1920 she had a major role in the film *The Black Spider*, also starring Roland Coleman. Lydia Kyasht finally settled in London and founded her own touring company, 'Ballet de la Jeunesse' in 1940. She died in London on 12 January 1959.

Edward Bainbridge Copnall, sculptor, 1903–1973

Copnall lived at 3a Greville Place from about 1937 to 1940. He was born in Cape Town in 1903, the son of a photographer. The family came to England and he trained at Goldsmiths College and the Royal Academy Schools. He began as a portrait painter but later turned to sculpture. An important early commission in 1934 was for the decorative sculpture and paintings at the new RIBA building in Portland Place. The following year he produced a set of carved panels for the Queen Mary. Copnall was president of the Royal Society of British Sculptors from 1961 to 1966 and his sculptures decorate many buildings in England.

[16]
Lydia Kyasht, who opened her first dance school in London in Greville Place

John Hutton, artist and glass engraver, 1906–1978

New Zealand-born Hutton developed a special technique for engraving on glass which he used with great success in many buildings in Britain, most notably the 90 glass panels he made for the great west front of the new Coventry Cathedral, consecrated in 1962. His technique gave engravings the graininess and shading of chalk drawings instead of the clear, restrained lines of traditional glass etchings. After being engraved, portions of the design could be polished with felt and emery paper to reduce opacity or give the illusion of depth. An artist who worked next door to Hutton shortly after the war recalled him as '*tall, handsome, somewhat saturnine. He worked endless hours; at whatever time in the morning I entered my studio I could hear John's drill whining. Sometimes, in between work, he strummed on his guitar*'.

Hutton subsequently engraved 37 glass panels for the first three floors of the Canadian National Library, which allowed natural light to reach the core of the building and provide illumination and a feeling of spaciousness. The panels took four years to complete. Between 1962 and 1968, Hutton submitted ten exhibits to the Royal Academy from 3a Greville Place, comprising studies and drawings for glass engravings on screens and panels. He was still there in 1970, but he died in Oxfordshire in 1978. His memorial service was appropriately held in Coventry Cathedral.

Dolf Rieser, artist, 1898–1983

Rieser is first shown in the telephone directories at 77 Hillsborough Court, Mortimer Crescent from 1947 to 1948. He then moved to 3a Greville Place, where he lived from at least 1950 to 1961. He later moved to Sumatra Road, West Hampstead, where he died in 1983. He is buried in Hampstead Cemetery. Born in South Africa of German Jewish parents, Rieser studied in Munich and Lausanne, gaining a doctorate in plant genetics. But he wanted to be an artist, and went to Paris to study engraving in the 1930s. His work was heavily influenced by his life in Africa, and he fused cave painting with surrealism. Rieser stood against the rise of Fascism in 1920s Munich and then in Paris, producing a folder of engravings with Miró, Kandinsky and others for the Republican cause in Spain in 1939 and another for Russia in the 1940s. Dolf fled Paris the day the Nazis entered the city and escaped on the last boat from Boulogne. Arriving in London he offered his knowledge of French and German to help the Special Operations Executive (SOE). After the War Rieser invented new techniques of colour printing and printing on plastic and laminates. He also wrote *Art and Science* in which he explored the parallels between these two sides of human activity. There are known to be over 400 editions of his prints, and numerous oils and watercolours throughout the world.

No.5 Greville Place, previously 11 Greville Place. Grade II listed

In 1836 this house was advertised for sale: 'A substantially-built detached Villa, with large garden, stabling etc., adapted for a family of the first respectability. Freehold. Let on lease to (George Brown) Robinson.'

William James Robson

Robson was at 5 Greville Place for less than a year before he fled the country. Advertisements in *The Times* offered a reward of £250 for information leading to his arrest: '*The said William James Robson was lately a clerk in the Transfer-office of the Crystal Palace, and is charged with a felony to a large amount*'. In October 1856 he was apprehended in Helsingborg, Denmark, where he was using the name Edward Smith. At his first court appearance in London on 10 October, Robson was described as 'gentlemanly-looking, very dejected and [to] feel acutely the unfortunate position in which his folly and extravagance had placed him'. He repeatedly tried to hide his face behind a large cambric handkerchief.

In 1853 Robson had been the chief clerk in the office handling Crystal Palace share certificates, whose owners left them in the care of the Company. In September 1855 it was discovered that certain shares had appeared on the market that should not have done. Robson invited a Company representative to his home in Kilburn Priory, where 'he would clear up the difficulty and put the matter straight at once'. Once they arrived, Robson almost immediately left the room. He never returned, and was not seen again until his arrest in Denmark. Robson told a police officer

> '*I hope they will not confine me for life in solitary imprisonment. I do not mind being transported, for I deserve it. I carried a ring about with me with prussic acid in it ..*
> *I intended to destroy myself .. I did not do it for fear of making my poor wife's latter days miserable.*'

Robson was charged on several counts of larceny and forgery. Despite his conversation with the police, Robson entered a plea of 'Not Guilty', which was later altered to a part plea of 'Guilty' to some of the charges. On 1 November Robson was in court for the last time, having recovered his composure and exhibiting a 'most confident bearing'. He was sentenced to 20 years' transportation for forgery and a concurrent sentence of 14 years for larceny. He arrived as a convict in Western Australia in 1858, but received a ticket-of-leave in October 1859 and a conditional pardon in November 1862.

DEVELOPMENT OF WIRELESS TELEGRAPHY. SCENE IN HYDE PARK.

(These two figures are not communicating with one another. The lady is receiving an amatory message, and the gentleman some racing results.)

[17] A 1906 Baumer cartoon from Punch

Lewis Baumer, artist, 1870–1963

Baumer was born in St John's Wood. He attended the Royal Academy Schools and began contributing cartoons and illustrations to the Pall Mall Magazine in 1893. He was most prolific during WW I and the years immediately following. A close observer of changing fashions, speech and habits, Baumer was hugely popular. His material appeared in *Punch* for 50 years [17]. He also illustrated several books and was well known for his portraits of young girls that appeared in the *Tatler* known as 'Baumer Girls'. He is shown at 5 Greville Place in directories from 1913 to 1940; he had moved to Bayswater by 1950.

No.7 Greville Place, previously 10 Greville Place

Demolished; site now occupied by four houses: No.7 Greville Place, Nos.28, 30 and 32 Greville Road.

Thomas Hill Mortimer, lawyer, d. 1853

No.7 dated from about 1827 and was probably built for Thomas Hill Mortimer,

Howard's solicitor, and accused by John Pocock of ruining his father. Mortimer lived at Greville Place until his death in 1853. Mortimer Road, Crescent and Place were all named after him.

Mortimer also had a prestigious London address: No.4 Albany Courtyard, Piccadilly. In 1802 plans were drawn up to convert the Piccadilly town house of the Duke of York and Albany into residential chambers, which became known as 'Albany'. In 1811 Mortimer leased the house's old kitchen space and offered to convert the rooms into a set of rooms. He was at pains to prove his suitability as a resident: '*Being by Profession a Solicitor and having understood an objection might arise to admitting me within the Precincts of the Establishment I think it necessary to add that my connections are but few and of the first Situation in Life, who generally expect me to wait on them, rather than attend me*'. He bequeathed the lease of his Albany Chambers to his son-in-law William Cole Long, 'in anxious hope' that Long, together with Mortimer's son Thomas, would take on his client list. Family members are buried at St John's Wood Chapel: it may be that Mortimer knew the neighbourhood, and influenced Howard's decision to purchase the Abbey Farm estate.

(here is Greville Road)

No.9 Greville Place (number unaltered). Building in 1830.

Henry Valentine Smith (known as Mr Swanborough), actor and manager of the Royal Strand Theatre, d. 1863

Henry Valentine Smith, or Mr Swanborough as he was known professionally, was an actor-manager who reconstructed and renovated the Strand Theatre in the Aldwych at a cost of £7,000 and reopened it in 1858 as the Royal Strand Theatre. He decided to star his daughter Ada in a series of burlesques written by H.J. Byron, *The Miller and his Men* and *The Lady of Lyons*. These proved very popular and the public flocked to see them. Henry had married Mary Ann Swanborough at St Clement Danes Church in 1829 and he decided to use her name professionally instead of Smith. Their five children all worked in the theatre.

In 1861 he was living at 7 Albert Terrace, Westminster. So he had not been living at Greville Place for long when he committed suicide there on 27 May 1863, by cutting his throat. At the inquest Frank Musgrave, his friend and musical director at the Strand Theatre, gave evidence. Musgrave was a lodger at Greville Place. He said Swanborough had recently had a fit and ever since, would sit for hours without speaking. When he did speak, he complained of giddiness and pains in the head. About this time, Swanborough, who had been deaf for 17 years and had always held out the hope he might recover, was told this would never happen. These events had made him very depressed. Musgrave also thought Swanborough's actions had been influenced by the fact that business at the Theatre was 'down'.

Anthony John Wright Biddulph

Biddulph lived at 9 Greville Place from at least 1871 to 1883. In a letter to *The Times* of 24 May 1875 about the Tichborne case, Biddulph said that he believed that the man claiming to be Sir Roger Tichborne was his cousin and he helped Dr Kenealy with his defence of the Tichborne claimant. It is interesting that Henry Dickins, the foreman of the jury (p 65), was his neighbour.

James Louis Garvin, editor of The Observer, 1868–1947

Garvin is shown at 9 Greville Place from 1909 to 1922. By 1923 he had moved to Great Cumberland Place. Garvin's parents were poor Irish Catholics who had left Ireland because of the potato famine and settled in Birkenhead. His mother was widowed when he was only two years old and he largely educated himself. He began writing on the staff of the *Newcastle Chronicle* and also contributed to the *Fortnightly Review*, moving on to the *Daily Telegraph* and to edit *Outlook*. Garvin was then hired to turn round the fortunes of *The Observer*, which under his management became 'the premier Sunday of its day' with a circulation of 200,000. Editor from 1908-1942, Garvin did most of his work from his study at 9 Greville Place; his biographer David Ayers wrote that 'the Observer office was, as far as he was concerned, an out-station of his study, where the paper was really edited'. Garvin was a keen family man; his daughters attended the nearby South Hampstead High School and his son went to Westminster. Garvin also wrote a four-volume biography of Joseph Chamberlain, and edited an edition of the *Encyclopaedia Britannica*. Churchill said of him: 'a friend of 50 years in whom courage, generosity and faithfulness shone in private and in public life as they shine in few'. Garvin died in 1947, at 'Gregories', Beaconsfield.

No.11 Greville Place, previously 8 Greville Place. Building in 1830

In 1839 the owner and occupier of the house, **John Carlon**, placed an advertisement in *The Times* for the sale of a carriage. Any replies were to be sent to his coachman.

> *To be sold, for £60, a very handsome lady's landaulet. The fittings up and repairs have lately cost £92 but the lady being deceased, it may be had a bargain.*

Carlon was a lawyer and small-time speculator on the estate. The first occupant of the house, he moved in about 1831, and owned both this property and the house next door, No.9.

Douglas Jerrold, writer and playwright, 1803–1857

Jerrold had moved from Circus Road St John's Wood only the year before when he died suddenly at 11 Greville Place on 8 June 1857, '*in the arms of his eldest son, and retained his intellect till within a few minutes of his death*'. The son of an actor-manager at the Sheerness Theatre, Jerrold taught himself numerous languages and immersed himself in literature. After two years in the navy, he began to write for a number of magazines. He had a horror of war, having seen wounded solders from Waterloo taken on board his ship. During the period 1821–1836, 51 of Jerrold's plays were produced at 13 London playhouses. The melodrama *Black-eyed Susan* ran for 400 performances; it made a fortune for the manager of the Surrey Theatre where it was originally produced, and the lead actor T P Cooke is said to have made the incredible sum of £60,000 for the performances he gave throughout his life. Jerrold however, received only £60 for the play, and he never made much money from his other writing. When *Punch* began in 1841, Jerrold was a constant contributor right up to his death, and as a salaried member of the *Punch* staff his financial situation was greatly eased. After his unexpected death, aged 54, his friends Charles Dickens and Thackeray organised performances which raised £2000 for his family.

Ascot Lodge

Nos.9 and 11 Greville Place were demolished and replaced by 'Ascot Lodge' in 1939. The block was subsequently purchased by Camden Council. In 1966 Miss Patricia Langham was found strangled in her flat. She ran the hair salons at the Ritz and Hyde Park Hotels and was known professionally as 'Miss Frances'. A gas fitter who had come to repair a water cistern was later convicted of her manslaughter.

Nos.13-19 Greville Place. Numbers as originally assigned. Built 1861-1862. Grade II listed.

In 1987, Nos.17 and 19 were up for sale with vacant possession, having been previously used as a residential home for the elderly.

No.13 Greville Place

C. W. Saleeby, MD, eugenicist, 1878–1940

Caleb Williams Elijah Saleeby was a writer and eugenicist. He is shown at 13 Greville Place in the directories from 1906 to 1939, having moved from Mandeville Place in Mayfair. Saleeby was first educated by his mother and then attended secondary school in Edinburgh, where he also obtained a first-class degree in medicine from the university. He practised briefly at a maternity hospital and the Royal Infirmary in Edinburgh, moving to London in 1901 to do postgraduate work. But he soon abandoned clinical practice to work as a freelance writer and journalist. A turning point came when he attended Francis Galton's famous lecture on eugenics at the Sociological Society in May 1904. Saleeby set out to popularise the new creed. He played a major part in setting up the Eugenics Education Society in 1907, but his outspoken views were soon at odds with the society's officers. He disagreed with their class prejudices and he also differed from most eugenicists in combining a concern for heredity with an interest in postnatal care and a desire to combat what he termed the 'racial poisons' of venereal disease, insanity, and in particular, alcohol. During WW I he became chairman of the National Birth Rate Commission and he moderated his earlier emphasis on eugenics as the salvation of the world. He also worked on the design of body armour and contributed to the invention of the steel helmet. After the war he threw himself into the campaign for cleaner air. He was an imposing and eloquent man, a popular and effective speaker. Throughout his life Saleeby worked tirelessly to combat disease, true to his family name which means 'crusader' in Arabic. He was often dismissed as a crank, but many of his causes had become more widely accepted by the time of his death, for example clean air legislation, preventative medicine, training in parenthood, and the dangers of tobacco and alcohol.

At the start of the War Saleeby left Greville Place and moved to Appletree, Aldbury near Tring, where he did unpaid consulting work in the local antenatal clinic. He died at his home on 9 December 1940.

No.15 Greville Place

Frederick Smallfield ARWS, painter, 1825–1915

Another of the estate's many artists who studied at the Royal Academy Schools, Smallfield was a good painter and etcher, best known for his figure subjects. Fellow students at the RA were members of the Pre-Raphaelite Brotherhood, and some of his work reflects their influence. Between 1866 and 1870, Smallfield sent five entries to the Royal Academy annual show from Greville Place, before moving his family to nearby Boundary Road. Smallfield was a founder member of the Junior Etching Club (1857-1864), which contributed to the revival of etching in England. Three of his children also became artists.

No.17 Greville Place

David Bomberg, artist, 1890–1957

Bomberg is shown to be living here in the 1939 and 1940 directories, having moved from Lymington Road. He was born in Birmingham, one of eleven children of Abraham Bomberg, a Polish immigrant leather worker, whose family kept an inn and reared horses. In 1895 they moved to Whitechapel and David was apprenticed to a lithographer in Islington. Evening classes given by Walter Sickert at the Westminster Art School had a major influence on his work. He also studied with Gilbert Bayes (later his neighbour, at No.4 Greville Place). In Paris he met Picasso and Modigliani. A loan from the Jewish Education Aid Society allowed Bomberg to attend the Slade School of Art from 1911 to 1913, where his fellow students included Paul Nash and Stanley Spencer. In December 1913 he exhibited with the Camden Town Group in Brighton and a year later he was a founder member of the London Group. He married Lillian Holt and his portrait of her is now in the Tate. He travelled to Palestine, Spain and to Russia in 1933 and later applied for a war artist's commission while living in Greville Place. Initially rejected, in 1942 he finally received commissions to paint a number of bomb stores. After the war he suffered further rejections and only got work as a part-time teacher at the Borough Polytechnic in London from 1945 to 1953. He was an excellent teacher, and his students included Frank Auerbach and Leon Kossoff. By 1950 he was at 12 Rosslyn Hill, Hampstead and during the 1950s he lived in Spain but when he became seriously ill in 1957 he returned to England, where he died at St Thomas's Hospital, London, on 19 August 1957.

EAST SIDE, from Maida Vale

Nos.2-20 even Greville Place, originally Nos.1-6 consec, 6a (two plots,) 6b, 7

Nos.22-24 Greville Place

No.2 Greville Place, previously No.1 Greville Place

Despite the fact that this was a semi-detached house, it was demolished about 1936 and the site is now occupied by part of Greville Hall. The other half still stands as No.4; the two houses were almost certainly a mirror pair.

On 24 June 1928 Mr **Ernest Ward Ravenscroft**, of 'Messrs Ede and Ravenscroft', died at 2 Greville Place. The firm, which is still in business, began trading in 1689 and is the oldest firm of tailors (specialising in supplying legal and academic robes) in London. In a codicil to his will, Ernest Ravenscroft directed that 'the business, stock, legal pictures and legal autograph books belonging thereto are to be sold to best advantage, giving the work hands a chance of obtaining the same...as I am the last of four generations of legal wig makers all born in the same house'. A retraction was rapidly published, saying that Ernest had made a mistake as the firm was very much in business, still making legal wigs, and run by his three brothers!

No.4 Greville Place, previously No.2 Greville Place

No.4 Greville Place [18] was recently offered for sale, erroneously described as 'a hunting lodge for George III'. Not only was Greville Place laid down in the open fields, but George III died in 1820, before the house was built. No.4a, in the style of a Dutch barn, was originally an artist's studio, probably built by Gilbert Bayes. The rear of the property is now a separate dwelling, numbered 4b.

John Angel, sculptor, 1881–1960

Angel lived at 4 Greville Place from about 1919 to 1927, before moving briefly to 57 Greencroft Gardens. He submitted nine works to the RA from the Greville Place address. Born in Devon he initially studied in Exeter before attending the Royal Academy Schools. Elected to the Royal Society of British Sculptors in 1919, much of his work was for war memorials – in particular at Exeter and Bridgwater. Angel married an American and the family emigrated to the USA in 1928. He produced many important pieces of work in America, including figures for the Cathedral of St John the Divine in New York, and the striking 10-ton statue of 'Francis Vigo' in Vincennes, Illinois. Angel died in Connecticut in October 1960, aged 78.

Gilbert Bayes, sculptor, 1872–1953

Bayes had previously lived nearby in 40 Boundary Road before moving to 4 Greville Place in 1930, where he built a new studio [19]. Born at 6 Oval Road, Camden Town, Gilbert was the son of a painter and etcher. Some 11 years later the family had moved to 21 Adelaide Road, near Chalk Farm. Bayes studied at the Royal Academy Schools where he won a gold medal and a travelling

[18] Exterior of No.4 Greville Place in 2005

scholarship, spending most of his time in Paris. His early works were mainly reliefs and equestrian statues, inspired by classical, medieval and Nordic mythology. He adhered to the ideals of the arts and crafts movement and developed an art deco style, gaining national prominence with his WW I memorials. Between the wars he experimented with modern materials, producing the frieze for Doulton House, Lambeth Embankment (now in the Victoria and Albert Museum). Other works from this period were the large-scale relief for the Saville Theatre (now a cinema) in Shaftesbury Avenue, depicting Drama through the Ages.

His best known work is the 'Queen of Time' clock above the main Oxford Street entrance to Selfridges, London. Commissioned by Gordon Selfridge and completed in 1931, the clock weighs 7 tons, and was soon being described by contemporaries as 'one of the sights of London'. Bayes also made a bronze plaque inserted in the marble floor below. Inscribed '*laid by members of this Store in admiration of him who gave it being*', the plaque has been damaged by the thousands of feet that have walked over it, but part of the artist's name is still visible. Bayes gained many prizes and was elected the president of the Royal Society of British Sculptors from 1939 to 1944.

He lived in Greville Place for over 20 years until his death in 1953, exhibiting over 30 pieces of his work at the Royal Academy. Bayes loved his garden, and in a letter written in 1945 concerning 'gardens of the future', he describes an idyllic afternoon in Greville Place 'lying in a hammock with white petals from the pear tree overhead falling like summer snow and with the birds enjoying a bath in a petal-covered pool a few feet away'. Bayes believed that more imaginative use should be made of water in English gardens. He installed a mosaic pool round his

[19] Drawing of Gilbert Bayes in his studio at 4 Greville Place

Doulton stoneware figure *Blue-robed bambino* at Greville Place. There were other stoneware decorations in the garden: a 'Diana' panel, ship finials and roundels decorating his studio wall. *The Lure of the Pipes of Pan* emerged from bushes in the front garden. The Doulton ornaments provided strong colour all year round, which Bayes preferred to planting flowers and weeding. Locally, Bayes' 1934 relief sculpture *Play up, play up, and play the game* can be seen on the boundary wall of Lord's Cricket Ground, while the rood in St Mary's Church Primrose Hill, is an earlier example of his work (1914).

No.6 Greville Place, previously No.3 Greville Place. Grade II listed

This is the only property hereabouts for which a leasing history (to 1913) has been established. It was first house to be completed in the road.

Fulk Greville Howard agreed to grant John Shackle (also spelt Shackel or Shakel) a 99-year lease of the plot in 1819, and he advanced £400 to Shackle to build the house. Shackle was another associate of George Pocock. The diary kept by Pocock's son John reports several visits between the families, and Mrs Shackle gave John a seal and watch-guard before he left London for South Africa. In 1833 Shackle granted a 21-year lease of the house to Daniel Horton, an upholsterer of Mortimer Street, off Cavendish Square. The grounds then included a stable and chaise house and a dung pit, poultry and dog houses. The inventory specifically mentioned that all the bedrooms had a 'Rumford Stove'. Four years later, John Shackle assigned Horton's rent to his brother Thomas, an Uxbridge brewer, to pay off debts. Shortly after this, a sale of the contents was announced:

> *3 Greville Place, July 1838*
> To auction on premises the nearly new handsome and modern furniture by Messrs Dowbiggin and Co, including zebra wood drawing room suite, with matching chintz curtains and a Wornum six and a half octave cabinet pianoforte.

When John Shackle died intestate in August 1857, probate was granted to Thomas, who arranged the sale of 3 Greville Place to George Foxley in 1859. Foxley, a decorator based in Princes Street, Hanover Square, paid £400 for the remainder of the 99-year lease. In 1891, Foxley's widow disposed of the lease to Soloman Barnett (see No.24 Greville Place) for £480. Barnett was an astute businessman, he sold on the property the same day to the Rev. Pengelley for £750, realising an immediate profit of £270! In 1913, the residue of the lease (only 6 years) was sold to Frederick Banbury, Fleet Paymaster in the Royal Navy, for £225.

Sir Anthony Burney, Chairman of Debenhams, 1909–1989

Anthony Burney lived at 6 Greville Place from at least 1971 to 1982. He was educated at Rugby and Cambridge. Burney became an accountant and was the chairman of Debenhams from 1971 to 1980. The house was advertised for sale in 1992 with an asking price of £795,000.

No.8 Greville Place, previously No.4 Greville Place

In 1887 the house was altered under the supervision of architect Robert Willey, FRIBA, of Ludgate Hill. He set up in practice in 1872 and worked in London, Middlesex and Kent. He was working for John Oulds, a retired oilman, who lived at No.8 for many years. Clearly, Oulds and other residents in the neighbouring Greville and Mortimer Roads were wealthy enough to use architects when refurbishing.

The 1950s Ordnance Survey shows the site as largely cle   l, with the remaining side wing described as a 'ruin'. A block of flats – Fi   .cis Court – was later built on the site.

Edward John Gregory RA, 1850–1909

Gregory is shown at 8 Greville Place from 1899 until his sudden death in 1909. Born in Southampton, Gregory started work in the drawing office of the P&O Steamship Company. He came to London to study at the South Kensington Art School and the Royal Academy Schools, and was employed on the decoration of a new museum which became the V&A. Gregory exhibited 34 pictures at the Royal Academy, more than half of which were portraits. His best known work is 'Boulter's Lock, Sunday Afternoon'. At the time there was a craze for boating, and the painting showed a busy scene on the Thames near Maidenhead. The painting took 10 years to complete and is currently in the Lady Lever Gallery at Port Sunlight. Gregory won gold medals at exhibitions in Paris, Brussels and Munich. He was president of the Royal Institute of Painters in Water Colours from 1898 until his death. One obituary described Gregory's 'kindly, retiring disposition' and noted that he had a bad stammer. He died in 1909 at his country home in Great Marlow, Buckinghamshire.

Reginald E. Higgins RBA ROI, artist, 1877–1933

Higgins lived at 8 Greville Place from about 1911 until his death in 1933. Born in Hampstead, he studied at the St John's Wood and Royal Academy Schools of Art. He began as a portrait painter and exhibited at the Royal Academy from 1900, but later became an illustrator of posters and magazines.

No.10 Greville Place, previously No.5 Greville Place

The first property on this site was described as a cottage with a well, mentioned in 1827 as the intended home for the Pocock family if their large Kilburn Priory property could be sold. It was demolished by 1833 if not before, and the plot remained as open ground until the mid-1850s, sometimes rented to nearby householders, presumably as an extension of their gardens. The house was built by George Duncan.

Alexander Maclean, artist, actor and playwright, 1867–1940

Maclean lived at 10 Greville Place from at least 1937 until his death in 1940. He initially worked as a barrister but abandoned the law and exhibited a picture at the Royal Academy in 1895. He was also a playwright and actor who toured with his own company. He died at Tonbridge aged 72.

(here is Greville Road)

Nos.14 and 16 Greville Place.

These two properties stand on what was originally a single plot, No.6a Greville Place. No.6a was shown as 'vacant ground' in the 1858 Rates. The two houses were listed as building in the 1861 Rates.

No.14 Greville Place

Henry Francis Dickins, draper, son of Thomas Dickins

In 1871 the census shows the younger Dickins at 14 Greville Place. He was the foreman of the jury at the Tichborne Claimant Trial in 1873/74. After the record length trial he wrote to the Treasury requesting payment of two guineas a day for the jury, but the Treasury would only agree the lower sum of £300. By the time of the 1881 census Dickins had moved from Greville Place to 7 Cavendish Road, Marylebone.

No.16 Greville Place

Mathilde Marchesi, teacher of singing, 1826–1913

Mme Marchesi died at her daughter Blanche's home in Greville Place in 1913. Born Mathilde Graumann in Frankfurt, she decided to use her musical talent to make a living after her father lost all his money. She studied singing with many famous teachers in Vienna, Paris and Milan and went on to become an accomplished performer. She wrote an autobiography, *Marchesi and Music*, published in 1897, which mentions almost every well-known person of the time. Her teaching methods were widely praised and many famous singers were among her pupils. Mme Marchesi had only recently come to live with her daughter in London; Blanche was also a well-known opera singer and teacher of music, practising her mother's vocal training system. She lived at 16 Greville Place from at least 1908 to 1921.

Hugh Godwin Riviere, artist, 1869–1956

Riviere lived at 16 Greville Place from about 1930 to 1940, having moved to Kilburn from Abercorn Place, St Johns Wood. He was the eldest son of Briton Riviere, an eminent painter from a long line of artists. Hugh was the honorary secretary of the Royal Society of Portrait Painters for many years. He painted portraits of several archbishops and bishops, and numerous noble and wealthy families. He died in 1956 aged 86.

Nos.18 and 20 Greville Place,
previously No.6 or 6b (18) and No.7 (20) Greville Place

The young John Pocock's diary incorrectly notes No.18 as built by George Pocock for his brother John. In fact, both properties were built by the *Carew* Brothers: Joseph was a stonemason and his brother John Edward was a sculptor. John Pocock bought or leased the house from Carew.

No.18 Greville Place, previously No.6 or 6b.
Also known as Greville Lodge. Listed Grade II

John Pocock, brother of George Pocock the developer, and uncle of John, the diarist.

The Rates show the house as occupied by Mr Carew from when it was newly built in 1828 until 1831, when John Pocock is first rated for the property. Pocock stayed for only a few years.

Samuel Statham Hope, silk merchant

A silk merchant, Hope moved to 18 Greville Place in the early 1900s from nearby Grove End Road. After his death, the entire contents were advertised for sale on 10 June 1914 by order of his executors. The contents of the house had been divided into several hundred 'lots', all meticulously listed in a catalogue, and ranging from small items such as hair brushes and pencil cases to furniture and carpets. The house was to be auctioned 2 days later.

No.20 Greville Place, previously No.7 Greville Place. Listed Grade II

Samuel Chappell, music publisher and instrument seller, c. 1782–1834

In July 1828, John Pocock Jr noted in his diary '*Mr Chappell of Bond Street ..wishes to buy a piece of our ground in Greville Hill*'. The house was completed by the following year and sold to Chappell for £1,400. The family lived there until Samuel died in 1834. The music firm of Chappell and Co began trading in 1811 at 124 Bond Street, when the following advertisement appeared in the Morning Chronicle:

Chappell and Co beg leave to acquaint the nobility and gentry that they have taken the extensive premises 124 New Bond Street and have laid in a complete assortment of music of the best authors, ancient and modern, as well as a variety of instruments, consisting of Grand and Square Pianofortes and Harps for sale or hire.

Samuel Chappell's partners were musicians John Baptist Cramer and Francis Tatton Latour. Beethoven wrote in a letter to his friend Ferdinand Ries that he had been told '*Chappell in Bond Street is now one of the best publishers*'. In the early 1820s the firm was awarded the Royal Warrant and in 1840 they began to make their own pianos. They later moved to 50 New Bond Street.

After Samuel's death, his widow Emily took control of the business, which was carried on by her three sons. Chappell and Co. are famous for organising the hugely popular series of readings by Charles Dickens in London, the provinces and America. He was a frequent visitor to the Bond Street store and praised the firm's handling of his tours:

Everything is done for me with the utmost liberality and consideration. Every want I can have on these journeys is anticipated and not the faintest spark of the tradesman spirit ever peeps out.

Emily Chappell moved from Kilburn Priory but kept the house, which was rented to a number of tenants, including the musician Frank Romer. The Bond Street shop still sold sheet music and pianos until November 2006, when it moved to Wardour Street, Soho.

Francis (Frank) Romer, composer, 1810–1889

20 Greville Place was Romer's home from at least 1859 until his death some 30 years later. In the 1851 census he was living in Harrington Street, Camden Town. Frank Romer was a musician and composer. He wrote several songs to Longfellow's poems, and he worked on operas with Mark Lemon (writer and colleague of Dickens); Lemon wrote the libretto and Romer the music. In 1866 Romer established a successful music publishing firm with Charles Hutchings. He died in Great Malvern in 1889. His son Sir Robert (Bob) Romer became a judge and married Lemon's daughter Betty in 1864.

In January 1966, the house was up for sale, advertised as ideal for 'home and income' as it comprised five flats, two of which were vacant. In August, a plan was submitted to Westminster Council to demolish and replace the property with a block of seven flats. This house was a mirror pair with No.18, whose owner James Sutton opposed the demolition. He wanted the two houses to be Listed and was supported by Hugh Pocock, a descendant of George Pocock. Both houses still stand.

Nos.22 and 24 Greville Place
(numbers as originally assigned)

Built in early 1860s, these houses were replaced by a block of luxury flats, 'Arncliffe', No.22 Greville Place. In January 1967, they were offered for sale on 99-year leases, with prices starting at £7,000 for a two-bedroom flat.

No.24 Greville Place

Soloman Barnett, builder and developer

Soloman Barnett was a builder and developer, living at 24 Greville Place in 1891. He was born in Poland about 1845 and became a naturalised British subject. His wife Florence was born in Plymouth, the daughter of a silversmith. Barnett was one of the neighbourhood's many Jewish residents and he developed a number of roads in Willesden, including Donaldson, Honiton, Lynton, Torbay, and Hartland Roads. In 1900, a meeting of local Jewish residents at his house in Brondesbury Road resolved to build a synagogue. Barnett sold them a plot of land he owned in Chevening Road at less than the cost price, and the Brondesbury Synagogue was opened there in April 1905.

[20] Greville Place Church c.1900, on the corner with Belgrave Gardens

Greville Place Congregational Church

In 1855 a group of Congregationalists who lived in Kilburn held their first prayer meeting in a room of a private house in St George's Terrace (later Belsize Road.) They moved from there to 1 Upton Road (later Belsize Road) and remained there, 'cradled in an artist's studio' until the Greville Place church [20] was opened in 1859, under Rev. Gallaway. A prospective minister could be invited by the members of the church to take a few 'trial' services before he was offered the post. A monthly church meeting was held and when a Congregationalist moved to Kilburn, the practice was to transfer 'membership' to Greville Place, following a letter of recommendation from the previous church attended. The records show that most members were local tradesmen or lower-ranked white-collar workers such as clerks, but a large number of servants also attended. John Leeds, who started Henley House School, worshipped here. The church closed about 1926.

The building was then adapted for use as a telephone exchange, first as 'Primrose Hill' and by 1930 as the 'Cunningham' Exchange. In 1971 the land was sold by the Post Office, described as 'the plot of a disused church'. It realised £100,500, equivalent to half a million pounds per acre. Zoned for residential development, the church was replaced by yet another block of flats. In 1975, the newly completed 'Lavington', No.24 Greville Place, offered luxury 2- and 3-bedroom units on 99-year leases, from £27,000 upwards.

(here is Belgrave Gardens)

GREVILLE ROAD (see map on p 70)

West of Kilburn Priory, the original name of this road was Springfield Road. The six houses east of Manchester Mews are listed in the 1851 census as Springfield Villas. Building began in the stretch between Kilburn Priory and Greville Place in the mid-1850s. The road name reflects that of the landowner, as do some of the house names. Many of the houses have been demolished, namely Nos.6-10, 16 even and Nos.15-33 odd. The road partly follows the line of a footpath that led across the fields to Kilburn Wells.

SOUTH SIDE, Nos.6-26

Previously Nos.1 and 2 Woolaston Villas, Nos.7-1 consec Eglinton Villas, Brignall House; next numbered as 2-20 even. Finally renumbered about 1884.

Woolaston is in Gloucestershire, Eglinton a village near Londonderry, and Sir Walter Scott wrote a poem called *The Brignall Banks*. The builder(s) may have had links to these places or loved poetry! Many of the advertisements for house sales mention the fact that this road enjoyed an elevated position.

(here is Kilburn Priory)

No.6 Greville Road,
previously No.1 Woolaston Villas, then No.2

In 1884, this 'well built residence' was up for sale on a 68-year lease, described as 'erected by an architect for his own occupation'. The current owner was leaving England. The house appeared again for rent in May 1902; the location was given as St John's Wood, close to bus routes and trains. It seems likely that **Marie Johnson**, painter of miniatures, was the new tenant. She exhibited at the Royal Academy in 1912 and 1913. In 1921 she married Frederick Salaman and from 1932 exhibited under her married name.

No.12 Greville Road,
previously No.6 Eglinton Villas, then No.8

In 1887, the artist **Otto Weber** was living here (see details under No.24).
In 1917 it was reported that **Mr Louis David Benjamin,** late of 12 Greville Road, had left just over £24,000 in his will. It included bequests to various Jewish charities. This neighbourhood, and more particularly the streets leading off the west side of Maida Vale, were home to many Jewish residents. Julia Frankau published her most controversial book in 1887 under her pen name 'Frank Danby'. Entitled *Dr Phillips, A Maida Vale Idyll*, it was a satire on Anglo-Jewish bourgeois society. Despite criticism, it proved a great success.

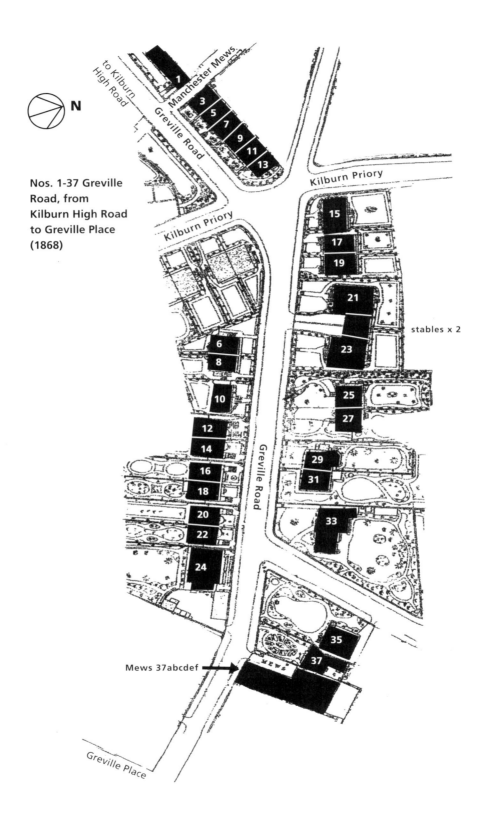

Nos. 1-37 Greville
Road, from
Kilburn High Road
to Greville Place
(1868)

stables x 2

Mews 37abcdef

Hilda Hechle, RBA, artist, d. 1939

Hilda Hechle won several medals while studying at the Royal Academy Schools. She specialised in Alpine landscapes but also painted portraits and was a talented illustrator. In the late 1920s Hilda moved from nearby Alexandra Road to 12 Greville Road, where she shared the house with her parents. When Hilda died in 1939, she was buried in the same grave in Hampstead Cemetery as her mother Una, (d.1931). Her father Henry John Hechle is also buried there.

No.16 Greville Road, previously No.4 Eglinton Villas, then No.12

The Times carried a list of war casualties daily during WW I, and on 6 October 1917 it included the name of 2nd Lieutenant John Leslie Barratt, Liverpool Regiment, whose father J W Barratt was a chartered accountant living at 'Calthorpe House', 16 Greville Road. 19-year-old John was educated at Oxford and was a member of the Volunteer Training Corps. He later joined the Artists' Rifles OTC and had been at the front since June. His commanding officer wrote to John's parents:

Your boy had just been with the battalion long enough to endear himself to us all, officers and men. On the night he was killed he was leading his platoon to reoccupy some ground which had been previously captured. He insisted on exposing himself in a most gallant manner, and unfortunately a sniper shot him dead. He had proved himself a popular and gallant officer.

Robert Kirland Jamieson, RBA, ROI, artist, 1881–1950 and his wife Dorothea Selous, artist

The couple moved to Kilburn in the late 1920s, probably from St John's Wood, moving on to Queen Anne's Gate by 1940. Robert was the son of a well-known Scottish artist, Alexander Jamieson. He started as an apprentice coach painter but decided he wanted to paint pictures, so went on to study art. From 1922 he was a regular contributor to the Royal Academy. A talented teacher, Jamieson was made principal of the Westminster School of Art in 1934. He died on 3 September 1950 in Crowborough. Dorothy Sealous was also an artist, a portrait painter.

No.18 Greville Road, previously No.3 Eglinton Villas, then No.14

In November 1867, the occupant of this house offered a £5 reward for the return of an item of jewellery: 'Lost, between Greville-road and Hyde-park, a gold necklet and carbuncle locket, acorn shape'.

Thomas Mutlow Williams, whip manufacturer

Just a few months before their neighbour's son was killed in the war, Thomas Mutlow Williams and his wife Louisa were in court, charged with 'an atrocious libel'. In February 1917, Mrs Williams had written a letter to the managing director of Vickers about one of the firm's employees named Percy Maxwell Muller whom she accused of being a German. 'It is shameful that our Englishmen, whose sons and brothers are fighting for us, should be insulted by having a German over them, and a grave danger in works employed by the Government.' Muller, a manager in the aeroplane works, was in fact a Scotsman, saddled with an unfortunate name at a time when England was at war with Germany. The contents of the letter had been circulated, and notices that Muller had put up in the works were defaced by unpleasant graffiti. Counsel said that Mrs Williams was an old lady '*and it was a pity she had not learned a little more sense'*. But she had apologised, so 'a farthing damages was sufficient'. The jury disagreed, and awarded Mr Muller £300.

No.24 Greville Road, previously Brignall House, then No.20

This was the first house to be built on the south side of the road, about 1855. In 1974 the entire property was Listed Grade II, but is incorrectly described in the Listing document as built by George Pocock in about 1819-25.

In the 1950s the house was progressively divided to provide three separate residences, Nos.24, 26 and 26a. The first division followed the death of Sir Goscombe John, when 'The Studio' was separated from the house. So for a few years the numbering was No.24 followed by No.26, The Studio; a further division created Nos.24, 26 and 26a by 1959.

(Carl Emil) Otto Weber, artist, 1832–1888

Weber was born in Berlin. He settled in Paris and became well known for his landscapes and animal paintings. He came to London in 1872, where Brignall House offered him great scope, as nearby stables enabled him to use live animals as models. He was a regular exhibitor at the Royal Academy from 1874 until his death in 1888. For Queen Victoria he painted a portrait of Prince Christian Victor, and two of her Skye terriers.

By 1887, Weber had moved to the smaller No.12 Greville Road. That year, his housekeeper Kate (Catherine) Marshall was sent for trial, accused of theft. The items in question were mostly household linen, valued at £30. When arrested, she admitted 'Yes, I took them and I am very sorry for it'. The police found 49 pawn tickets related to the stolen property in her room. She had previously been in Weber's employment at No.24. Weber died the year after, at 32 Great Ormond Street, after a long illness.

Edwin Roscoe Mullins, sculptor, d. 1907

Mullins moved his young family to 24 Greville Road in 1887 from Fitzroy Street, 'even then, a move so far from the centre was a bold enterprise'. He followed fellow sculptor Weber at the house, and he sent 11 exhibits to the Royal Academy from this address, including several busts.

His most unusual work was a circus horse in the Brighton cemetery in 1893 for Mr Ginnett, a well-known circus owner. Mullins moved to Finchley some time after 1902 and died in Walberswick, Suffolk in 1907. His wife exhibited handicrafts but was better known as a pioneer in the field of progressive educational thought. She was a co-founder of King Alfred School, Golders Green.

Sir William Goscombe John, sculptor, ARA, RAI, 1860–1952

Goscombe John moved into 24 Greville Road after fellow sculptor Roscoe Mullins left. William was born near Cardiff in 1860, the son of Thomas John, a woodcarver employed in the workshops set up by Lord Bute for the restoration of Cardiff Castle. As a young man William assumed the name Goscombe from the name of a Gloucestershire village near his mother's home. He trained in Cardiff and then in London, and from 1884 at the Royal Academy Schools. He travelled widely in 1888 and 1889 in Italy, France, Greece and Egypt. The RA's gold medal and a travelling scholarship allowed him to travel in 1890 to Spain and Africa and to take a studio in Paris, where he studied with Rodin. Goscombe John settled in St John's Wood in 1892, and then moved to Greville Road in 1904, where he stayed for the rest of his life. His sculpture was influenced by artists such as Sir Alfred Gilbert. He was recognised as a highly skilled artist and his work was in great demand. Goscombe John worked in both bronze and marble and produced numerous public statutes, such as that of Edward VII (Cape Town) and the Marquis of Salisbury tomb in Westminster Abbey, but probably his best-known work is the 'Drummer Boy' in Liverpool (1905). He also produced a bronze bust of neighbour Sir Frank Dicksee for the Royal Academy. Goscombe John was knighted in 1911, and as a patriotic Welshman he was given the freedom of Cardiff in 1936.

He continued to exhibit at the Academy for over 60 years. An academic sculptor first and last, Goscombe John was out of sympathy with the modern style that appeared when he was in his prime. A friend wrote:

He deplored what he called the 'Easter Island' sculpture of the moderns ... In old age he was something of a recluse, living alone except for his housekeeper. He was a kindly figure with a somewhat elfin quality, usually reclining among his many objets d'art and smoking innumerable small cigars. He was fond of the garden but not of gardening, and in recent years his main concern was his studio – filled with plaster busts of many Victorian and Edwardian celebrities – which had been bombed and lay useless for nearly eight years.

This damage was caused by the flying bomb that fell on the other side of Greville Road, in the back garden of North Hall, in 1944.

Goscombe John outlived many of his artist friends and died at his home in 1952, aged 91. He is buried in Hampstead Cemetery [21], in the same grave as his wife.

No.26 Greville Road

Willi (Wilhelm Josef) Soukop, RA sculptor, 1907–1995

In the 1950s Soukoup was living close by in Alexandra Road and he had moved to The Studio, No.26 Greville Road by 1954. He was still at this address in 1982. Educated in Vienna and apprenticed to an engraver, Soukop came to England in 1934, where he taught at Dartington Hall and other schools. After he moved to London in 1945 he became a teacher at the Bromley and Guildford Schools of Art. He produced a number of sculptures for new schools around the country and for LCC housing estates. In 1961, an aluminium figure by Soukop was one of several 'striking exhibits' in the garden of Keats House, Hampstead, part of an open air sculpture show by artists living in the Borough. His work is in many

[21] This bronze statue marked the grave of Goscombe John and his wife Marthe, who died in 1923. It is based on work for an earlier memorial to Lady Ellen Webb. The statue was stolen in 2001 and although it was recovered, it has recently been stolen again, from a store in Finchley.

museums in England, America, and Europe. In 1995 the house was advertised for sale with a 40-foot artist's studio.

No.26a Greville Road

In 1965, No.26a was offered for sale, described as a 'delightful period house… full of possibilities'.

Nos.28-32 even, Greville Road

These are built on the redeveloped plot of the original No.7 Greville Place.

NORTH SIDE, Nos.1-37 odd

No.1 Greville Road
Nos.3-13 odd, previously 1-6 consec Springfield Villas (renumbered 1884).
Nos.15-37 odd: some early houses named or numbered as part of Elm Bank; next, numbered as Nos.1-23 odd, finally renumbered about 1884.

No.1 Greville Road

From the mid-1860s, No.1 Greville Road provided a place of worship for a small group of Catholic priests newly arrived in the neighbourhood, and they remained until the Sacred Heart Church was opened in Quex Road.

The premises were later shared by several organisations, the longest lived being the **Kilburn Provident Medical Institute and Dispensary** until 1939. Established in 1875, a small weekly fee was charged to become a member: in 1903 it cost $1\frac{1}{2}$ d for adults and 1d for children. The end of year report recorded the total number of members as 4,426. 4,641 persons had been treated and 1,389 home visits had been made. In 1906 the local press announced that Dr Davson of 203 Maida Vale was retiring. He had served the Kilburn Provident Medical Institute since 1880. A handsome pair of silver candlesticks was presented to him 'by poorer patients attending the Institute'; over 200 of them subscribed to the cost of the gift. He was succeeded by his son.

In 1902, the **Kilburn Recreation Club for Working Girls** hired rooms from the Medical Institute. Membership was open to all, but aimed at Jewish girls over school age: one night of 'drill' plus singing, dancing, games and reading were provided.

No.1 was briefly home to the **Hampstead Public Vaccination station** and a **YMCA,** and for somewhat longer to a **St Johns Ambulance Station.** Reflecting the times, when any household that could afford it had live-in help, **the Metropolitan Association for Befriending Young Servants (Mabeys)** also had a branch here, which survived until the 1920s. Begun in 1875 and based in Great College Street Westminster, its object was 'to befriend young girls from 13 to 20 years of age who are in or entering domestic service, and are exposed to peculiar dangers and difficulties from the want of home protection'. In 1886 it was reported that it in the preceding year they had assisted over 6,000 girls to find jobs and homes.

In the 1901 census, Alfred Dan, aged 34, was shown at 1 Greville Road. He was a draper who had a shop at 10 and 10a Kilburn High Road. In 1895 he had undertaken a partnership for the shop with Owen Owen, a Welsh businessman who had a large department store in Liverpool. Although Dan paid the rent regularly there were problems. Owen managed to obtain £1000 from Dan in 1905, but he still lost another £3000 on his investment. The shop remained empty for the next six years.

(here is Greville Mews originally Manchester Mews. No original buildings remain.)

Nos.3–13 odd Greville Road are still standing.

No.9 Greville Road, previously No.4 Springfield Villas

On 24 July 1853 the death of a 3-year-old 'daughter of a gentleman' at this address was reported by the Registrar General. She had died of cholera in just 24 hours.

(here is Kilburn Priory)

All houses on the Greville Road frontage between Kilburn Priory and Mortimer Crescent have been demolished.

Nos.21 and 23 Greville Road

These two houses were linked by a stable block. Both properties were schools for many years; this was a scholastic 'corner' with a vengeance, as St John's School, Kilburn College, the London College of Divinity and Henley House School were, at various times, just over the back garden wall in Mortimer Road.

No.21 Greville Road, previously No.7 Greville Road

Rev. Boultbee, first principal of the London College of Divinity, occupied this house for a while. The College moved away in 1866 and No.7, then called 'Cleveland House', became a collegiate school run by John Julian Frederick Cuttance; in 1871 and 1881, the Census showed 13 and 9 male pupil boarders. By 1882, it was the Kilburn Collegiate School, later renamed the North Western Collegiate, run by J R Waddlelow. By 1889 the college had departed, and the house was up for rent. The interior of the property had clearly suffered from its many years as a school: '*This house is now being thoroughly repaired and an intending tenant will be able to choose papers, tiles etc*'. There was a billiard room, and the description concluded: 'the rooms in this house are exceptionally fine'.

No.23 Greville Road, previously No.9 Greville Road

In the 1860s and 1870s this was a school run by Miss Elizabeth Richardson and later Benjamin Richardson, variously called Elm Bank House, Elm Bank School, and latterly St Albans (and International) College for Ladies. In 1872 it was described as a 'college for daughters of professional men' and as 'St Albans' in 1874, under the direction of Mme Bouchais, with an impressive list of tutors and a 'liberal table'. By 1881, the school had been in business for 20 years and pupils could now study in England, France or Germany. Modern languages, music, drawing and painting were specialities. Physical activities were also provided, from swimming to riding and callisthenics. The 1881 Census shows Benjamin as headmaster, with twelve girl boarders and a couple of resident tutors. The school had moved out by 1882.

In 1908, this house and the adjoining stables (No.23a) were valued for mortgage purposes. Miss Azulay (see below) then had a yearly tenancy of the 10-bedroom house, while the coach house was separately rented to Mr John Clare Saul. The application stated that the property was held on a 94-year lease, granted in March 1858. The estimated sale value was £900.

Miss Gertrude Florence Azulay, pianist, teacher 1870–1961

Gertrude Azulay was a respected performer and teacher. Born in Islington, she studied at the Guildhall School of Music and was living in Lambeth with her grandparents in 1891. They moved to Kilburn, where Gertrude opened 'The Kilburn Conservatoire of Music' at 4 Kilburn High Road, in December 1893. The family probably lived 'over the shop', as her grandfather Bondy Azulay is shown at the same address. Her grandmother died in 1895 and Bondy three years later. By July 1899 Gertrude had moved the school round the corner to 23 Greville Road.

Gertrude performed at charitable events for Jewish causes throughout her professional life, including several concerts before the Conservatoire was opened. One was arranged by Mrs Herbert Bentwich, whose husband was a member of the Jewish intellectual group 'The Wanderers of Kilburn'. Arthur Davis, who lived at No.25 Greville Road, was also a member. The London Zionist League and the West London Zionist Association held meetings at the Conservatoire. Herbert Bentwich and Israel Zangwill attended in 1899, Isaac Snowman in 1905 (see 192 Alexandra Road p 109).

Professional and amateur students studied the 'Russian method of pianoforte' at the Kilburn Conservatoire. An 1897 advertisement stated 'Piano, violin, singing and all musical subjects are taught by an eminent staff of professors'. Miss Azulay later added elocution classes and took resident pupils at Greville Road. Her students gave regular concerts at the Steinway Hall, Lower Seymour Street and in 1894, one was held locally at Kilburn Town Hall, Belsize Road. In 1909 reviews praised the London debut of 10-year-old 'wonder-child' Effie Kalias, who had been studying for 4 years under Miss Azulay. Effie's 'extraordinary musical, intellectual and technical development' was noted and she was acclaimed as a 'musical genius'.

Pupils were given individual attention at the Conservatoire, and home tuition had been added to the services on offer by 1910. The school was a great success and needed larger premises as well as better transport links. It had left Greville Road by April 1913 and reopened as the 'School of Pianoforte' at 2 Goldhurst Terrace by February 1914. This address had the added benefit of being near the Finchley Road Metropolitan Railway Station, but by 1918 the school had relocated to 2 Swiss Terrace, Swiss Cottage. In the 1920s, Miss Azulay was appointed a professor at Trinity College of Music, London, and opened more schools in other areas of London. By the end of the 1920s the 'Hampstead Centre' had moved yet again, to 10 Buckland Crescent, where Miss Azulay was still listed as a teacher of pianoforte in 1939. After a long life, Gertrude died in a nursing home in 1961, aged 90. At the time she was living at 41 Marlborough Place. Her funeral was at the Spanish and Portuguese Jews cemetery in Hoop Lane, London, her ancestors being Sephardic Jews.

No.25, previously No.11 Greville Road

Arthur Davis, engineer, Jewish scholar, 1846–1906

Davis was born in Derby and entered the family business as an engineer and manufacturer of mining apparatus. Shown in the 1881 census at 20 Abbey Road, by 1891 he had moved to 25 Greville Road, where he stayed till at least 1895. Davis was a member of a group of Jewish intellectual professionals, 'The Wanderers of Kilburn'. Other members lived nearby: Israel Zangwill and Asher Myers in Oxford Road on the Willesden side of the High Road, and Israel Abrahams in Birchington Road. During the 1880s they met at each others' houses 'in and about the half-bohemian area of Kilburn and St Johns Wood', to hold discussions about Anglo-Jewry: a key question being what constituted Jewish identity in modern society. They played a leading role in developing Zionism. Davis, his daughter Nina Davis Salaman and Zangwill produced an important translation of the Mahzor, a Jewish prayer book.

Davis died in Torquay, having never fully recovered from a serious operation a few months previously. His obituary described him as '*an earnest and pious Jew, deeply attached to the "old paths" and greatly disinclined to religious innovations, a fine type of the non-professional religious scholar*'.

No.27 Greville Road, previously No.13 Greville Road

In 1888 this property was advertised as 'well adapted for elderly people or an invalid'.

Emma Frederica Newbery, founder of Homes for Blind Children, d. 1902

Emma was the daughter of Colonel Newbery. In 1871 she was living with her widowed mother in Northam Villa, Randolph Road. Emma moved to 27 Greville Road about 1899, where the 1901 census shows her with her sister Charlotte, both single and living on their own means. Emma's obituary said: '*She conducted for many years the Home for Blind Children at Kilburn and succoured many helpless ones*'. (For details of the Homes, see under Springfield Lane).

No.29 Greville Road, previously 15 Greville Road

Robert Spence, artist, 1871–1964

Born in Tynemouth, Northumberland, Spence was the son of an amateur etcher and water colourist. He studied at the Newcastle School of Art, the Slade and in Paris. Spence moved to Kilburn from Kensington about 1907 and is shown at this address until 1940. He was awarded the Croix de Guerre in 1918, but we were unable to discover the reason. Spence was a historical painter of scenes and people and exhibited 21 pieces of work at the Royal Academy during his years at Kilburn. He had moved to 9 Frognal Gardens by 1951 and remained there until his death in 1964. He appears to have been a successful artist and left about £180,000 in his will.

No.31 Greville Road, previously No.17 Greville Road. Also known as Rock Villa

The original lease for the land dated from 1852 and was granted to Ferdinand Ball (see Mayfield, Mortimer Crescent, p 89). The house was built about 1854, and the second occupant was Frederick Joseph Mavor, a veterinary surgeon, who stayed for over 20 years. In 1867 he won a court case against the freeholder General Upton and his neighbour, concerning the height of a wall, which they claimed Mavor had built in contravention of his lease. The case was dismissed as 'unnecessary and frivolous'. Frederick was the son of William Mavor, also a veterinary surgeon. In the 1830s, W. Mavor and Son were based in New Bond Street and in 1851 the family were living in Hornsey; the census shows that Fredrick's elder brother, Alexander, was also a vet. By 1891 Frederick had left Kilburn for Hendon. The 7-bedroom house was for sale in 1911, with 39 years to run on the lease.

No.33 Greville Road, previously No.19 Greville Road. Also known as Greville Lodge

This house was for sale in 1865 and again in 1867. The advertisement shows it to have been one of the very best houses on the estate, with an 83-year lease to run. The property appears to have been home to a succession of wealthy stockbrokers.

Kilburn, Greville-lodge, 19 Greville-road, a detached family residence standing in its own grounds of good extent, with large conservatory and a double range of forcing-houses. The grounds are tastefully disposed with lawns and flower beds, and planted with rare shrubs and trees, which prevent the property from being overlooked. The residence is of modern erection and stands in one of the most salubrious suburbs of town.

In addition to the usual bed and reception rooms, the accommodation included a 'lofty ladies' sitting-room', a china closet and both wine and coal cellars.

(here is Mortimer Crescent)

No.35 Greville Road, previously No.21 Greville Road. Also known as Howard Lodge

No.35 Greville Road was offered for sale in 1931, the particulars describing an 'old-world' residence, with a 'charming' walled garden. The lease had about 20 years to run.

Charles Goodhart, actor, d. 1910

Charles Goodhart, his wife Alice (also an actress) and young son are shown here in the 1901 census, but had left by 1904. Goodhart was an acquaintance of Oscar Wilde. During the early stages of his trial for indecency, Wilde bumped into Goodhart in Piccadilly Circus. As his name was displayed in every newspaper and heralded by every newsboy, the embarrassed Goodhart began to speak of the weather. Wilde, never one for hypocrisy, immediately interjected 'You've heard of my case?' and added 'Don't distress yourself. All is well. The working classes are with me... to a boy.'

After working for the Primrose League, Goodhart went to Ceylon as a tea planter and only became an actor on his return to England in 1891. He was a member of Mr Benson, Mr Lewis Waller and Mr Bourchier's companies and his first London stage appearance was under Waller, in Wilde's *The Ideal Husband*. Goodhart committed suicide just before Christmas 1910 by cutting his throat at his lodgings in the Camberwell New Road. At the time, he was playing at the Palace Theatre, Camberwell. A fellow actor and friend Ernest Leicester told the inquest that Goodhart had been unwell and acting so strangely he'd been evicted from two sets of lodgings. A doctor had been called, but Goodhart told him it was 'very imperative' he played his part that evening, and the doctor gave him a 'draught' so he could go on. Goodhart had been in poor health for some years and more recently, experiencing frequent hallucinations. The accidental death earlier in the year of his brother-in-law Nathaniel Cooke, had also upset him greatly.

No.37 Greville Road, previously No.23 Greville Road. Also known as Milford Cottage

In 1854, the house was leased from builder Ferdinand Ball (see also No.31, above) for £750. In 1881 and again in 1912 the sale of 'The Chalet, otherwise No.37 Greville Road' was advertised. It was listed Grade II in 1974 and is currently known as Regency Lodge, something of a misnomer as the house is Victorian.

Nos.37a, b, c, d and e Greville Road

By the 1860s, there was a small mews on this site. A succession of OS maps from the mid 1860s to about 1913 show three and then four properties (one was subdivided), with a glassed-over area at the far end. Some rebuilding and alterations had occurred by the 1930s. By the mid-1950s, all the buildings had been demolished, apart from one reconfigured property on the Greville Road frontage, numbered 37b. Today three smaller houses, Nos.37c, d, and e, have been built behind 37b. These were advertised for sale in 1963 as 'three delightful little modern houses in leafy cul-de-sac', each on a 71-year lease.

A number of artists lived at 37a and 37b Greville Road, which appear to have been converted into studio/living accommodation in the early 1930s.

No.37a Greville Road

Alfred Frank Hardiman, RA, FRBS, sculptor, 1891–1949

Hardiman lived at 37a Greville Road from about 1933 to 1940, when the house and one of the studios took a direct bomb hit. After this he moved his family to Stoke Poges in Buckinghamshire. He reopened the remaining London studio after the war and was shown in the directories at 37b Greville Road in 1949. 'An earnest man with acquiline features', Hardiman was born in Holborn, the son of a master silversmith and showed his first sculptures at the Royal Academy in 1915. He enlisted in the Royal Flying Corps later that year, serving as an engineer's draughtsman until the war ended. He resumed his studies after the war and won a scholarship to Rome, where he developed his style based on classic Roman and Greek sculpture. On his return to London his bronzes were exhibited at the Royal Academy; one was bought by Stephen Courtauld and is now in Eltham Palace. Monumental and architectural sculpture came to dominate his work.

While he helped transform the sculptural face of London between the wars, Hardiman is best known for his controversial equestrian statue of Earl Haig in Whitehall. The first model was commissioned in 1929, but was criticised by Lady Haig as a poor likeness of her husband. A second model in 1931 was attacked for its poor representation of the horse and a lack of protocol in depicting the Earl without a hat. The statue was finally unveiled on 10 November 1937, the day before the anniversary of the Armistice. It cost £9000. Lady Haig refused to attend the ceremony, saying her husband would never have ridden such a horse. Amusingly, it was said the position of the hind legs of the horse suggested urination, not movement! Supporters argued it was a good, modern work, combining a representational figure with a stylised horse and cloak. Hardiman argued it had not occurred to him to study a real army horse, as he was a sculptor not a photographer. Gilbert Bayes, Hardiman's neighbour in Greville Place (p 62), was so unimpressed by the final statue that he modelled two alternative versions in plaster. A large hoarding was subsequently erected behind the statue in Whitehall, advertising whisky, with the words 'Order Haig and don't be Vague'. After many objections, it was replaced by a poster for Dewar's whisky.

Hardiman was awarded a silver medal for the statue of Earl Haig by the Royal Society of British Sculptors, but papers were later found which showed the controversy had badly affected both his finances and his health. Hardiman died of cancer in 1949 aged 57.

No.37b Greville Road

Albert A. J. Houthuesen, artist, 1903–1979

In 1938, Houthuesen succeeded fellow artist Arthur Ewan Forbes-Dalrymple, who had been at 37b Greville Road for a few years only. Houthuesen was born in Amsterdam, the eldest of four children. The family moved to London in 1912 following the death of his father. Houthuesen later said his mother 'struck her husband on the head with a shoe – a blow from which he died'. They lived first at 7 then 20 Constantine Road, Hampstead, where Albert attended Fleet Road School. The family was desperately poor: Albert described his Hampstead childhood as all 'penny-pinching and pawn shops'. But his artistic skills, with support from the Rothenstein family, enabled him to obtain a scholarship at the Royal College of Art. Here he met painter Catherine Dean: they married in 1931 and lived at 20 Abbey Gardens. In 1938 they moved to 37b Greville Road but were bombed out in 1940.

Unable to make a living from his paintings, Albert gave evening classes. Rejected as unfit for the army, during the war he worked in the drawing office of the North Eastern railway company in Doncaster. During his absence from London, over 40 oil paintings stored in a neighbour's cellar were destroyed by damp. This, together with the tedium of tracing engine designs, led to a nervous breakdown. In 1952, the couple returned to London, to 5 Love Walk, Camberwell. Houthuesen remained largely unrecognised until 1961, when he had his first one-man exhibition in London. His expressionist, colourful paintings often featuring the recurring themes of the sea or clowns, are now in the British Museum, Tate Gallery, V&A, Ashmolean and many other museums. Houthuesen died at his Camberwell home in 1979, after long periods of ill-health.

Douglas Wain-Hobson, sculptor, 1918–2001

During his brief time at 37b Greville Road (1952–1954) Wain-Hobson hit the headlines. In 1953, his statue *Recovery* (not his choice of title) – a life-size bronze of a naked man with prominent male genitalia – was placed outside St James's Hospital, Balham in south London. Locals considered raising his fee of £500 and returning the statue to him. 'No man would want his wife or daughter to see it' was the comment made by one outraged resident.

Brought up in Sheffield, Wain-Hobson had little formal education after he left school aged 11. But he could draw, and won scholarships to the Sheffield College of Art (where he became interested in sculpture) and then the Royal College of Art in 1938. He joined the College staff in 1953, teaching and working alongside Jacob Epstein, Henry Moore and Edward Paolozzi. His most notable commission was probably the huge figure of Shakespeare at the Shakespeare Centre, Stratford-on-Avon (1964). He entered and was tipped to win the 1953 International 'Unknown Political Prisoner' competition arranged by the ICA, but the commission went to Reg Butler. Wain-Hobson retired in 1983 and died in Macclesfield, Cheshire. His statue of the naked man survived all the criticism; it remained in place until St James's closed in 1988, when it was moved to St George's Hospital, Tooting.

George Him, illustrator and graphic designer, 1900–1982

George Him (born Himmelfarb) moved into 37b Greville Road after Wain-Hobson left. Educated in Warsaw, Moscow and in Germany, George originally studied philosophy. He worked in Germany and Poland before coming to London in 1937. As a book illustrator and graphic designer, he did much of his work in partnership with Jan Lewitt, including the creation of *The County of Schweppshire* (words by Stephen Potter) and illustrations for the well-known children's book *The Little Red Engine*. They also designed the 1951 Festival of Britain 'Guinness' Clock in Battersea Park; 25 feet high, it included three synchronous clocks, nine reversible electric motors and took 5 months to build. To the delight of large crowds, every 15 minutes the clock went through a 4½-minute routine, featuring well known characters and animals from Guinness advertising.

George Him was devoted to Israel and its causes. He designed the large Masada exhibition (1966) and worked for many years as a design consultant to El Al Airlines. He was a large, bear-like man whose bulk contained a generous heart; *Who's Who* listed his recreation as 'work'. George was living in Greville Road at the time of his death.

(here is Greville Place)

No.39 Greville Road

The directories show that in 1928 the horse dealers Mortensen, Mouritz and Peter, were at this address, just over the estate boundary. However, 3 years later the motor garage, the 'Carlton Engineering Company', was at this address, reflecting social changes and the switch from horses to motorcars.

7 Mortimer Road and Mortimer Crescent

n 1854, Mortimer Road was being constructed across land leased to the estate agent and developer Ferdinand Mercer Ball. The road between Greville Road and Kilburn Priory was called Mortimer Road. The short road built to connect with Alexandra Road was later named Mortimer Crescent, although houses here were still sometimes listed under Mortimer Road by name and/or number, or differentiated as 'the Crescent, Mortimer Road'.

In 1915 residents suggested that Mortimer Road be renamed Greville Crescent, while Mortimer Crescent should stay as it was. The LCC did not agree, and the names were in fact changed to what they are now: Mortimer Crescent (all the way from Greville Road as far as the present Langtry Road) and Mortimer Place (from Mortimer Crescent to Kilburn Priory).

MORTIMER ROAD, EAST SIDE (see map on p 83)

The houses were numbered 1-2, 3a, 3b, 4-12 consec Mortimer Road, later Mortimer Crescent.

Six named houses, later Nos.13-18 consec Mortimer Crescent.

Four original houses remain on this frontage, Nos.7 and 6 (with a modern side addition numbered 5) and Nos.17 and 18 (with a later side extension). All other properties are post-WW II rebuilds.

WEST-SOUTH SIDE (see map on p 83)

None of the original houses remain. Some of the largest properties on the estate were built here. Set in spacious grounds, they occupied slightly elevated ground, originally looking across to the London & Birmingham Railway line. These were named as part of Mortimer Road and later numbered in Mortimer Place or Mortimer Crescent.

No.6 Mortimer Crescent, previously No.6 Mortimer Road

Arthur Lett, architect, 1846–1895

Lett was an architect who lived here during the 1880s. Locally, he was responsible for the buildings of the St Lawrence's Institute, Glengall Road in 1891, which later became the Kilburn Polytechnic. By 1892 he had moved to 138 Abbey Road, his address at the time of his death.

No.9 Mortimer Crescent, previously No.9 Mortimer Road

Arthur Turrell, historical engraver

Turrell was living here in the late 1870s and at the time of the 1881 census. He was one of the most prolific engravers of the period, and based his work on contemporary artists. He exhibited six engravings at the RA between 1877 and 1890. By 1891 the family had moved to 38 Cavendish Road. His son Arthur James also became an artist, specialising in etchings. He lived locally, in Alexandra Road and later Chatsworth Road, Willesden.

Mortimer Road and Mortimer Crescent (1868). No. 192a Alexandra Road was built in the late 1890s

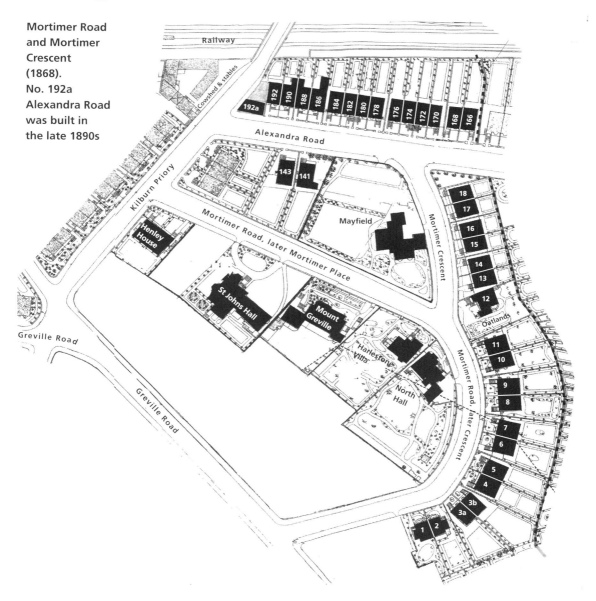

No.10 Mortimer Crescent,
previously No.10 Mortimer Road

Harry Jarvis Cave, builder

Harry Jarvis was one of four sons of Edward Jarvis Cave, a speculative builder. The family speciality was mansion flats and they are responsible for many blocks in West Hampstead. Harry was living in Mortimer Road in 1895 but soon moved away. In November 1903, *The Times* reported his bankruptcy hearing, when he was living in Lauderdale Mansions, Maida Vale. He told the court he had begun business about 10 years previously when he was 21 years old, and had since built in Clapham, Willesden Lane, Haverstock Hill, and Maida Vale. Cave ascribed his failure in part to his inability to let many of the flats he had built in Lauderdale Road.

No.10a Mortimer Crescent, previously Mortimer Road,
comprising the ground and basement floors of number 10

George Orwell, author, 1903–1950

Orwell is best known for his novels *The Road to Wigan Pier* (1937), *Animal Farm* (1945) and *Nineteen Eighty-Four* (1949). 10a Mortimer Crescent was one of several Camden addresses where Orwell lived. Orwell (real name Eric Blair) moved to Kilburn from nearby Abbey Road in 1942, renting the lower half of the house. Anthony Powell said that its Victorianism delighted Orwell:

The house conjured up those middle-to-lower-middle-class households … on which his mind loved to dwell .. 'They would probably have kept a Buttons here,' he said, enchanted at the thought … The sitting-room with a background of furniture dating from more prosperous generations of bygone Blairs, two or three 18th century family portraits hanging on the walls, might well have been the owner's study in a country house.

Not everyone saw Mortimer Crescent in the same light as Orwell. Comments about a *'remarkably dreary… icily cold…damp basement flat'* were made by friends and acquaintances. The boiler would go out if someone didn't get up in the night to stoke it. Unfit for active war service, Orwell was working for the foreign service of the BBC, and then became the literary editor of an independent Socialist paper, *The Tribune*. He and his wife moved to Islington in 1944, forced to leave Mortimer Crescent by a bomb falling in the garden of North Hall that June.

After the War and the death of his first wife, Orwell moved to a remote farmhouse on the island of Jura. Here he collapsed with tuberculosis after producing the first draft of his long-planned novel. He was treated with the new drug, streptomycin, obtained from the USA with the help of his friends David Astor and Aneurin Bevan, but this was abandoned after painful side-effects. Rested, he returned to Jura where he sat in bed and typed the second draft. He collapsed again when he had finished it. *Nineteen Eighty-Four* was published in 1949. Much misunderstood, it was a Swiftian satire of the time, not a serious prophecy of a particular date. Still ill, Orwell was in a sanatorium in Gloucestershire for most of 1949, before transferring to University College Hospital in London. The doctors gave him some hope although they knew there was none, and he married for a second time in October 1949. His friend Anthony Powell noted that despite the 'tragic circumstances of Orwell's failing condition' the marriage 'immensely cheered him.' Orwell died in January 1950.

No.12 Mortimer Road, previously Oatlands

Annie Besant, social reformer, author, 1847–1933

While by no means as grand as the mansions opposite, Oatlands was a detached house, on a larger plot than the neighbouring houses. The social reformer Annie Besant [22] lived here between 1876 and 1883. In her lifetime, she campaigned for justice and freedom in many areas of life, from marriage, motherhood and contraception to working conditions, education, politics and poverty.

Annie was born in 1847 in the City of London, the daughter of William Wood, an underwriter working in the City who died when Annie was only 5 years old. When Annie was about 9, Ellen Marryat (the wealthy sister of Captain Frederick Marryat, author of boy's adventure stories) offered to educate her, and Mrs Wood agreed. Annie stayed with Miss Marryat at her private school in Dorset until she was 16. She returned to her mother with an unusually good education for a girl of that time. She was also deeply religious and very unworldly. It was hardly surprising that after a very brief acquaintance, Annie married Rev. Frank Besant in 1867, when she was just 20 and he was 27. This proved to be a dreadful mistake. She later admitted 'I drifted into an engagement with a man I did not pretend to love'.

Frank believed a wife should be submissive and not question her husband's decisions, but Annie was a clever woman with ideas of her own. After her baby daughter nearly died in 1871, Annie's religious faith was severely shaken. The couple moved to Sibsey in Lincolnshire where Frank was appointed vicar. Annie turned for sympathy to Charles Voysey, who had a theistic church in London. When she was encouraged to write a pamphlet that her husband feared could put his living at risk, he gave her an ultimatum to take communion regularly in Sibsey or leave. Annie chose to go. She moved to Norwood in South London with her young daughter Mabel in 1874, while her son Digby stayed with her husband.

It was a hard time: Annie had no work and very little money. Society was critical of a woman who had left her husband and at one point Annie had to take in 'fancy needlework'. She began to be interested in the Freethinkers, who believed everyone had a right to think for themselves. In 1875, Charles Bradlaugh, an atheist and president of the National Secular Society, gave her a job as a writer under the pen-name 'Ajax' on the freethinking newspaper, *The National Reformer*. He also encouraged her to give public speeches and, unlike Frank, treated her as an equal. An

[22]
The social reformer Annie Besant

attractive woman with a beautiful voice, Annie quickly became very popular and filled halls around the country. For the next 11 years Bradlaugh and Annie were close and affectionate friends. They were generally thought to be lovers, though this was never admitted.

Annie moved to Mortimer Road probably to be near Charles Bradlaugh, who is shown in the 1881 Census as a widower at 20 Circus Road. In 1877 they attempted to publish the American Charles Knowlton's pamphlet on birth control and were instantly arrested and prosecuted for obscenity. At the time, sex was never publicly discussed and marriage meant a series of pregnancies for most wives. At the trial on 18 June 1877, Annie, conducting her own defence, was the first woman to publicly endorse 'checks' on conception to help relieve poverty. Bradlaugh and Besant were found guilty and sentenced to 6 months' imprisonment plus a fine of £200. However, the Court of Appeal overturned the sentence. Annie then published her own advice, *The Law of Population*, in 1878, which sold thousands of copies. But the public thought her shameless, and that year Frank Besant succeeded in an action to reclaim Mabel, on the grounds that Annie's views made her unfit to bring up a young girl. Eventually Digby and Mabel were reconciled to their mother.

From 1884 Annie's life was full of incident, but it took place away from Mortimer Crescent. She started a literary magazine, George Bernard Shaw introduced her into the Fabian Society, of whose executive she became a member, upsetting Bradlaugh who by this time had become an MP.

In 1888 she wrote an article about the appalling conditions of girls working at Bryant & May's match factory in Bow. With the powerful title of *White Slavery in London* it gained widespread attention. Annie wrote that the girls, working very long hours, paid only four shillings a week and their health badly affected by yellow phosphorus which destroyed their jawbones, were effectively slaves, supporting the large profits of the company. Three of the women who spoke to Annie were sacked, so she helped them organise a union and they went on strike. After three weeks the company agreed to their conditions and the strike ended. The Matchgirl's Union was the first union for women.

She then became interested in the Theosophist Society and put her large house at 19 Avenue Road, St John's Wood at the disposal of Madame Blavatsky, one of its founders. Inspired by the philosophy emanating from India she moved there and after some years in educational work became a member of the Indian National Congress Party and ultimately, in 1917, its president after 3 months in prison for her outspoken attacks on the British Government in India. However, she disagreed with Gandhi's method of passive resistance. In 1929 she retired from politics and as president of the Theosophical Society, and in 1933 died in Adyar.

Frederick Beesley, gunmaker, d. 1928

The 1901 Census shows Fredrick Beesley living at 12 Mortimer Road. He was a former employee of Purdey, the famous gunmakers, who applied his invention of a spring action for guns. In 1879 he set up his own gun-making business at 2 St James Street. When he died in 1928, his son H P Beesley took over the firm. Beesley guns are now highly prized collectors' items.

Catherine Isabella Dodd, author, 1860–1932

Catherine Dodd was a teacher, headmistress and lecturer; she was also an educational pioneer who believed children benefited from beautiful surroundings. Her small Manchester school was decorated with Morris wallpaper with painted furniture to match. Subjects were not taught in isolation; instead, links were made wherever possible.

She retired in 1920 and by 1921 was living at 12 Mortimer Crescent, where she stayed until her death in 1932. She began writing, initially for children, as 'the leisure occupation of her years of retirement'. In 1925 she published *The Farthing Spinster*, which was well received. One reviewer said *'like Mr Galsworthy's Forsyte Saga, it is a family history covering several generations. Delightful – there is no more applicable word'*.

At her death she left the considerable sum of £16,463, including bequests of £100 to Miss Edith Wilson of Oxford and £200 to Professor Alexander of Manchester, both with the same curious caveat: 'In the hope that she/he will utilize this sum or part of it in paying for taxicabs'.

No.13 Mortimer Crescent, previously Severn Villa

Leopold Farmer, local estate agent and auctioneer

Farmer [23] had moved here by the mid-1880s, probably from the nearby (and far less prestigious) Holtham Road, where he was living in 1881. Holtham Road led west out of Abbey Road and was originally called Albert Road, but has been obliterated under the post-WW II clearances. Born in Jamaica, Farmer established his estate agent's business in 1877 and played a major role in Kilburn's development. He became a vestryman and local councillor and was still at 13 Mortimer Crescent in 1919. His office, L. Farmer and Sons, is shown in directories at 12 Kilburn High Road until 1908, when it moved to 61 Kilburn High Road (between Oxford Road and Cambridge Avenue) staying there until at least 1936.

During WW II the Council tried to ensure that houses did not stand empty, so when 13 Mortimer Crescent was damaged by the flying bomb that landed in the garden of North Hall in 1944 the Council agree to pay £350 to repair it, provided that the owner would reoccupy the house as soon as work was finished. A month later, repairs were still incomplete but the Council was told that three people were already living in the basement, while the owner plus six other persons were intending to move in as soon as the rebuilding of the flank wall was completed.

[23] Leopold Farmer, estate agent and auctioneer, a major player in Kilburn's development

No.16 Mortimer Crescent, previously 'Cherwell'

Belle Bilton, Lady Dunlo, music-hall actress, d. 1906

[24] Belle Bilton, music-hall star of the 1880s, who became Lady Dunlo

In the summer of 1890 the entire country was intrigued by a court case concerning the divorce of Lady Dunlo, who before her marriage was known as Belle Bilton, a beautiful star of the music halls [24]. At the time of the court case, Belle was living at Cherwell House. She was the daughter of John Bilton, a clerk in Walworth, South London. With her sister, Flo, Belle first appeared as 'The Bilton Sisters', performing a popular song and dance act in music halls up and down the country. When Flo got married, Belle continued to perform. Unfortunately, she met an American con-man called Alden Weston and became pregnant by him just as he was sent to goal for conspiracy and fraud. Fortunately, Belle had a wealthy young admirer, Isidor Wertheimer, grandson of a successful art and antiques dealer in New Bond Street. In July 1888 Wertheimer rented a house in Maidenhead and arranged for a doctor to deliver Belle's child. He then took a large house at 63 Avenue Road for Belle's use.

The following year the young Lord Dunlo became besotted with Belle whom he met at a club, and they were soon married (July 1889) at the Hampstead Registry Office. Dunlo's father Lord Clancarty was furious, tried to have the marriage annulled, and when this failed sent his son to Australia, leaving Belle to fend for herself. He then hired private detectives to watch her and Wertheimer, and once the detectives had provided him with evidence of an affair, he persuaded Dunlo to sign divorce papers and return to England. Dunlo seems to have been genuinely in love with Belle but was forced to obey his father because he had no income of his own. As far as the public were concerned it was a case of the beautiful actress and her husband the young Lord, against a wicked old Earl trying to destroy the marriage of the happy couple. It was also about class differences.

At the 5-day trial the detectives, a somewhat inept family firm, said they had seen Wertheimer and Belle together at the music hall and at the Avenue Road house. This weak evidence was quickly discredited by the defence counsel. There was no proof that Wertheimer and Belle had ever been lovers, the judge and jury did not uphold the divorce and within days, Lord Dunlo and Belle were reunited. Less than a year after the trial (May 1891) the Earl of Clancarty died, Dunlo inherited and became financially independent. Dunlo and Belle had four children and remained happily married until Belle died of cancer in December 1906.

No.18 Mortimer Crescent, previously 'Coniston'

Laurence Evelyn Wood Pomeroy, motoring writer and consultant, d. 1966

Pomeroy joined his father, chief engineer to the Vauxhall and Daimler companies, as his personal assistant. He worked on high-performance problems in cars, especially supercharging, and joined the staff of *The Motor* in 1936, where he became editor until he founded his own company in 1958. His articles and technical papers 'could be relied upon to be witty, informed, trenchant and controversial'. 'Pom', as he was known, wrote a two-volume history, *The Grand Prix Car* and a third was in preparation at the time of his death. He also collaborated with Stirling Moss to produce *Design and Behaviour of the Racing Car*. He lived here from about 1964 until his death.

Charles Douglas-Home, editor of *The Times*, 1937–1985

Born in London, Charles was the youngest son of Henry Montagu Douglas-Home, an ornithologist who was known as the BBC's 'bird man'. His uncle was the Tory Prime Minister, Sir Alec Douglas-Home. Charles Douglas-Home lived at 18 Mortimer Crescent for many years, from at least 1969 until his death on 29 October 1985. After diplomatic work in Kenya, he entered journalism with the *Daily Express*. In 1965 Douglas-Home was appointed defence correspondent for *The Times*; he followed the sound of the guns in the old tradition of war correspondents, reporting from the front line of the Six Day War in 1967 and the Soviet invasion of Czechoslovakia in 1968. In 1966 Charles, or Charlie as he was known, married **Jessica Violet Gwynne,** an artist and stage designer. He rose through the ranks of *The Times* to become its editor in 1982, a period of great difficulty after Rupert Murdoch had taken it over. After becoming editor, Douglas-Home contracted bone-marrow cancer, but continued until his death to edit through a telephone amplifier which relayed his voice from the Royal Marsden Hospital to *The Times* conference room.

Mayfield Cottage, later No.19 Mortimer Crescent

Ferdinand Mercer Ball, major leaseholder in Greville Estate, c.1819–1904

Mayfield Cottage was the home of Ferdinand Mercer Ball, probably built to his design and completed by 1859. Born about 1819 in Ryde on the Isle of Wight, in the 1851 census he was living at 17 Garway Road in Paddington as a rate collector and Benefit Building Society secretary. Ball was a major leaseholder on the estate and his substantial house was a 'cottage' in name only. It occupied probably the largest site on the property, with frontages on Mortimer Road curving round the Crescent to Alexandra Road, but there are no pictures of what the house looked like. Before moving into Mayfield Cottage, Ball lived in Greville Road and in one of the smaller houses in Mortimer Road. He left the Cottage in the early 1870s and by the 1881 census he had retired and returned to the Isle of Wight. He died there, aged 85, in 1904.

After Ball left, the property was occupied successively by two stockbrokers and renamed more appropriately as just 'Mayfield'. They were succeeded by **Mortimer Saul Woolf** by April 1900, and the family remained at the house until the death of his widow, Miriam Woolf, in 1929.

Mortimer Saul Woolf OBE, food manufacturer, 1857–1926

Woolf was born of English parents in New York. By 1881 the family had returned to England and were living in Marylebone. Described in successive census returns as a merchant, a manufacturing chemist and employer, and food product manufacturer, Woolf was living with his wife and young family in Acol Road by 1885, at 16 Greville Place from 1895 to 1899, and then at 19 Mortimer Crescent.

The family's company was called Yeatman, founded by Mortimer's father Edward Woolf, in 1857. Based in Denmark Street, it later moved to Watford. In 1897 it became Yeatman and Co., with Mortimer as Chairman. The annual report for 1898 reported 'sales show a steady increase over the previous year, and in aggregate are the largest ever made since the existence of the business'. This success may well explain the family's move from Greville Place to the much larger 'Mayfield'. Yeatman made and marketed an eclectic mix of household products from concentrated ginger beer and lemon squash, custard powder, table jellies and cordial, to curry powder, malt vinegar, pickled anchovies and liquid ammonia.

Mortimer's younger son Walter was one of the thousands of young men who died in WW I: *'from wounds received the previous day'* reported *The Times* of 30 September, 1915. Mortimer's eldest son Edward became a distinguished surgeon and wrote a letter from Mayfield in 1909 concerning the establishment of a Jewish Hospital. He was also part of the family business, taking over the Chair from his father. Not surprisingly, he took a special interest in the health of his employees, who apparently referred to him as 'Mr Teddy'. He died in 1957.

Hillsborough Court, Mortimer Crescent

This was one of the first sites on the estate to be privately redeveloped as a block of flats. The unusually large site allowed 122 flats to be built, replacing Mayfield, which had been a single family home. Hillsborough Court was formally opened by Hampstead's mayor, Alderman Newman, on 2 November 1934. The architect was R J H Minty (who was involved in developing seven other blocks in London at the time.) His 'neo-Tudor' design incorporated a special feature: 'by means of balconies each flat has a separate approach and corridors are unnecessary'. A year later *The Times* carried an advertisement for the block, described as 'London's latest Miracle Building'. Rents from £91 to £110 per annum inclusive would secure 'one of the finest bachelor flats in Europe'. There were many up-to-date features: an entirely enclosed bed recess, shower, and private telephone exchange. An incongruity was the inclusion of an inglenook fireplace, in addition to the central heating.

A year later the block was again advertised as offering the 'ideal luxury flat for bachelors or married people', with constant hot water, tiled kitchen including a large electric refrigerator, lift access and the services of a day and night porter. Yearly rents ranged from £91 to £130, at a time when many nearby houses were lacking basic sanitation let alone the luxury of central heating. Today, a two-bedroom flat in Hillsborough Court can sell for £250,000 or more. The main entrance carries the building date of 1934, and a shield motif with a stag's head and Tudor roses.

No.61 Hillsborough Court, Mortimer Crescent

Baroness von Hutten, writer, 1847–1957

Appearing here only once in the 1940 directory, Bettina, Baroness Von Hutten, was the author of at least thirteen novels written between 1907 and 1935. She used several pseudonyms, including Betsey Riddle and Sacha Gregory.

She was born Bettina Riddle of Irish-American parentage at Erie, Pennsylvania in 1874. When she was 17 she paid her first visit to Europe and began writing for the *English Illustrated Magazine*. Her family settled in Florence and there she studied music. She considered opera, but her overriding ambition was to become an author. After her marriage in 1897 to Baron von Hutten zum Stolzenberg, she devoted herself to writing at her home in Schloss Steinbach, Bavaria and produced her first novel. *Pam* was the story of a charming and original heroine from childhood to womanhood. The treatment was unusual and the book created a sensation.

Bettina's marriage ended in divorce in 1907. She moved to England, where she considered a stage career. She was beautiful and charming, and her height (she was nearly 6 feet tall) added to her striking appearance. In 1909 she played Aunt Imogen in *Pinkie and the Fairies*, but is not mentioned in the review in *The Times*. Bettina's real love was story writing. Her popularity increased with each novel, she made a great deal of money and spent it recklessly. WW II brought an end to her success, as no one wanted to read books written by someone thought to be a German. Given her married name, Bettina was treated as an enemy alien and forbidden to travel more than 5 miles from her home. She ignored this restriction and was summonsed in 1916, fined £5 and 5 guineas costs.

Bettina had an affair with Charles William Harmsworth, Viscount Northcliffe. She then married the actor Henry Ainlee and their daughter Henrietta Riddle was briefly engaged to the broadcaster Alistair Cooke in Cambridge, about 1932.

Bettina again made money after the War, when her books came back into fashion. But her extravagant spending continued and in 1925 a receiving order was made against her. Due to recurring ill health her appearance in the Bankruptcy Court was delayed until April 1930, at which time she was living in Chelsea. Her honest and straightforward manner was commended and she was discharged. Bettina regained her American nationality in 1938 and after her stay in Kilburn lived in California until 1948. Subsequently she returned to Europe and died in London in 1957.

North Hall, later No.20 Mortimer Crescent

North Hall was built at the curve of the road, where Mortimer Place now meets Mortimer Crescent. In 1860, Mr George Brown put out to tender the job of building a 'carcase' of a house in Mortimer Road; he may well have purchased the land from Ferdinand Ball. The architects were Flexman and New, and the tender accepted was for £1,173, from builders McLennan and Bird. The house was completed in 1861 and enjoyed an unusually large garden. Like its neighbour St John's Hall, North Hall also boasted an Italianate tower. George Brown was described in the 1871 census as 'a manufacturer of interior decorations', at which time he employed 35 men and boys. He also owned seven of the smaller houses in Mortimer Road and Mortimer Crescent, and had probably retired by the time of the 1881 census, which simply records him as a 'gentleman'.

In September 1878, Mr and Mrs Brown were among several hundred day trippers aboard the 'Princess Alice' paddle boat, which was rammed and sank in the Thames. George survived, but his wife was drowned. Another local resident also died (see Kilburn Baths, p 22).

Ignatz Boskowitz, a fur and skin merchant, rented North Hall for a couple of years after 1883, while Brown moved into one of his smaller houses: 'Oatlands' just across the road, recently vacated by Annie Besant (see p 85). Brown returned to his old home for a short time and then left Kilburn. A few years after moving he died at Cricklewood Lodge in January 1892. His properties, including North Hall, were progressively disposed of. By late 1891, it was **Ernest Callard**'s new home. Born in Marylebone, Callard became a baker and confectioner like his father and also expanded into catering.

Callard was succeeded by a publisher, and then North Hall stood empty or had a few short-term tenants. In 1907 a property in Mortimer Road was selected as 'excellent in every way' for another home, this time for Jewish patients suffering from incurable tuberculosis. The property was surveyed, an architect was engaged to make alterations, the lease was ready to be signed, but at the last moment the neighbours objected. Their opposition was 'so formidable' that the owner refused to let the property. It seems likely that North Hall (or possibly Mayfield, then home to a well-known Jewish businessman) was the house in question.

Sidney Hartnoll Beard lived at North Hall for a few years after 1918. Beard was the founder of 'The Order of the Golden Age', an organisation with Christian roots, advocating the 'adoption throughout Christendom of a bloodless and natural diet'. He wrote a number of books on the subject, including one with the attention-grabbing title of *Is flesh eating morally defensible? A Comprehensive Guide-Book to Natural Hygienic and Humane Diet.*

John Spedan Lewis bought the remainder of the North Hall lease for just over £14,000. He lived there from 1925 to 1930, and also owned the house opposite, 6 Mortimer Crescent, which was used as staff quarters. His father was John Lewis, founder of the department store. The extensive grounds surrounding North Hall enabled Lewis to indulge his life-long love of natural history and wild animals. An 'owlery' was built to house his collection of pheasants and owls (managed by a Mr Gander!) as well as various animal enclosures and a kennel run. Spedan Lewis financed expeditions to collect rare species, which he bred in captivity and gave to zoos. In 1927 and 1928, he wrote in the *Gazette*, his firm's house journal:

'The Birds at North Hall. I have here a small collection of birds which are, for the most part, rather exceptionally interesting. To see them properly takes about three-quarters of an hour or a little more. The birds can be seen without going through the house, so visitors in this way need not have any fear of causing inconvenience'.

Employees were asked to make an appointment, and friends, 'especially children' were welcomed.

Spedan Lewis also collected wild animals. A colleague described what happened during regular games of tennis at North Hall:

He had a tennis court made with cages at each end in which he kept lynxes. One of those cages was up against the back netting so if you went to pick up your ball, there was a lynx about a foot away.

In 1929, John Lewis moved his family and menagerie from Kilburn to Hampshire. North Hall and 6 Mortimer Crescent (the 'cottage') were put up for sale by the John Lewis Company in 1932. The details give some idea of the scale of the property.

Very quiet situation: sunny aspect: good garden and first-rate hard tennis court, billiard room, panelled drawing room (patent dancing floor), panelled dining room, fitted library. 7 bed rooms, 3 bath rooms, electric light; central heating; drains all recently put into perfect order; garage for 2 large cars; cottage opposite divided into maisonette for 2 married servants.

Buyers may have been thin on the ground, and the company next tried to develop the site. A proposal was made in 1933 to replace the main house with seven smaller ones, and although the authorities were inclined to give permission, instead the house was reported as sold in January of the following year, for just under £3000.

The last occupants were the poet and playwright **John Drinkwater** and his wife **Daisy Kennedy**. The house was convenient for Regent's Park, where he played in productions at the Open Air Theatre in 1933 and 1934. He died in his sleep at North Hall, on 25 March 1937. His obituary noted that Drinkwater *'had watched the Boat Race and had been in the evening to a party at which some members of the crews were present; and excitement, following on much hard work, proved too much for his heart'*.

North Hall was unoccupied and being used by the Council as a temporary furniture store when it was badly damaged by a V1 flying bomb in 1944. The site was subsequently cleared and now forms part of the Mortimer Estate.

Ernest Callard, baker and confectioner, d. 1929

It is possible that Callard's grandfather was also in the bakery business. Ernest's business prospered: in 1896 three separate firms amalgamated to form Callard, Stewart and Watt, with Ernest as one of the managing directors. The firm held the royal warrant as 'bakers and confectioners to the Queen' and had shops in Bond Street, Piccadilly and Regent Street. Ernest picked up other directorships and became a wealthy man; in 1901, the census shows him staying at the Metropole Hotel, Folkestone, where a fellow guest was the Marquis of Headfort. Callard left North Hall in about 1905. At the time of his death in 1929 Ernest was living in Sussex, but his cremated remains were buried in Hampstead Cemetery, Fortune Green Road, in the same grave as his newborn son Douglas, who had died in 1891. Callard left just over £40,000 in his will. His wife and daughter are also buried at Hampstead.

[25]
Spedan Lewis
(© John Lewis
Partnership
Archive
Collection)

John Spedan Lewis, businessman, founder of John Lewis Partnership, 1885–1963

John Spedan Lewis [25] was born in 1885 and spent his childhood in Hampstead, at Spedan Tower, his father's mansion overlooking the Heath at Branch Hill. He was a pupil at nearby Heath Mount School and went on to Westminster. Rather than go to college, Spedan Lewis joined his father's firm aged 19; when he and his brother Oswald were 21, they both became full partners in the business.

Spedan and his father held decidedly different views on business. Spedan began to develop his 'Partnership' idea: to share running of the business and profits among members of staff. In 1914, his father gave Spedan control of Peter Jones, a failing draper's shop in Sloane Square. Spedan began implementing his ideas by setting up 'committees for communication' between staff and managers, When his father threatened to terminate Spedan's partnership at the main Oxford Street shop, Spedan agreed to exchange this lucrative post for sole control of Peter Jones. By 1919, he had increased its annual turnover five-fold, to £500,000. His success both impressed his father and brought about a reconciliation: 'That place is a great credit to the boy – a very great credit!' The Partnership scheme went ahead. Spedan believed women had an important role to play in running his business, and his wife Sarah Beatrice Hunter joined the company as a trainee. She shared her husband's ideals and became the Partnership's first Deputy Chairman. John Spedan Lewis died in 1963.

John Drinkwater, dramatist and poet, 1882–1937

John Drinkwater started his working life in the offices of the Northern Assurance Company, where he worked for 12 years. He left to start an amateur theatre company with a friend, who later provided the financial backing for him and his first wife Cathleen to turn the company into a professional one, and build the Birmingham Repertory Company theatre. The opening production in 1913 featured the couple as Malvolio and Olivia's maid Maria in *Twelfth Night*. He wrote biographical plays of Abraham Lincoln (1918), Mary Stuart (1922), and Oliver Cromwell (1923). He directed Laurence Olivier and Peggy Ashcroft in his play *Bird in Hand* in 1927. Drinkwater established himself as a respected poet and playwright, but much of his later work failed to match the quality of his earlier writing. He died at North Hall in March 1937.

Daisy Kennedy, musician, d. 1981

Drinkwater's second wife was Daisy Kennedy, a talented violinist. Born in Australia, she studied music in Adelaide, Prague and Vienna before coming to London. Her successful career included the first public performance of several violin works. In 1924, Drinkwater was named in Daisy's divorce from her first husband, pianist Benno Moiseiwitsch. Divorce was then a messy and often public process. A note Daisy wrote to Benno was produced in court saying that if Benno visited the Metropole Hotel Brighton he could obtain the necessary evidence for a divorce (presumably by consulting the hotel register). A waiter from the Metropole confirmed that Daisy and John had stayed at the hotel. The divorce was granted on the grounds of Daisy's adultery, and although she implored Moiseiwitsch to be allowed to keep her two children, custody was given to her ex-husband. John and Daisy married later that year; she outlived Drinkwater by 44 years, and died in 1981.

MORTIMER ROAD

St John's Hall and Mount Greville or Greville Mount
(later one building and renumbered as 4 Mortimer Place)

The two houses in the 1857 engraving [26] are shown soon after they were completed. These are the only large properties in the road for which detailed pictures exist. The house on the right with the Italianate tower was 'St John's Hall'. The house on the left was variously called Greville-mount or Mount Greville, but is shown in the engraving as 'The St Johns Foundation School', which in fact occupied both properties at the time.

St John's School was founded in 1851 by Ashby Blair Haslewood, vicar of St Mark's in Hamilton Terrace, St John's Wood, and set up in the house next to the church. Haslewood wanted to offer free education for the sons of poor clergymen and also to provide a choir for the church. The wealthy parishioners of St John's Wood responded positively, votes were cast to select the most deserving pupils and the first eight boys began their studies in January 1852. The headmaster was Rev. Anthony Francis Thomson, curate at St Mark's. However, Haslewood soon fell out with the management committee, the parishioners and eventually his bishop and the local MP. Haslewood had contributed £4,000 towards the building of St Mark's church, which he regarded as a loan to be repaid through pew rents. Everyone else considered it a donation, and parishioners believed he had set up the school in order to get the curate's stipend paid by the church rather than himself. The school committee therefore rented Greville Mount House in Mortimer Road (about a third of a mile away and outside Haslewood's parish) and moved the school, and Thomson, there in 1854.

An advertisement in *The Times* for 5 January 1857 listed Reverend Anthony Thomson as the headmaster at Greville-mount House and St John's Hall, Mortimer-road, Kilburn and claimed the school equipped the pupils for 'the Army, Navy, Civil service, India and university. The Foundation is exclusively for the sons of Clergymen of limited income, who pay £45 p.a.' By 1857 there were 30 scholars. Thomson found it difficult to cope financially. He had initially received £50 per pupil per year, out of which he had to find all their food and accommodation, but this amount was later reduced to just £40 a head. In 1854 he asked the committee for an advance. In October 1857 he wrote requesting a leave of absence 'in consequence of the state of my pecuniary affairs'. The request was refused, but Thomson ignored it and left. The committee had no option but to dismiss him. Thomson later moved to Avranches in France and was Chaplain at Dinard, when he died in 1885. He was the author of *The English Schoolroom* (1865) and *The Milestones of Life* (1866). In February 1863 he wrote to *The Times* from Avranches pointing out that Robert Romer (son of the musician Frank Romer), the senior wrangler of Trinity Hall, Cambridge, had received his education at St John's Hall, Kilburn (see Frank Romer, p 67).

With Thomson's abrupt departure the school was in trouble. At the end of 1857 the 30 boys left Kilburn and joined a school in Walthamstow. Then in 1859 the

[26]   Mount Greville and St John's Hall, Mortimer Crescent (*Illustrated London News*, 1857)

school took a lease on Clapton House in East London. On 29 June 1869, it was reported that thanks to an anonymous benefactor, the St John's Foundation had bought a site in Surrey for £2,500 and planned to build a school for 100 boys at a cost of £16,000. In August 1872 the school made its last move to Leatherhead, the present location for the independent school of 450 pupils (142 boarders, and with 53 girls in the 6th form). Past pupils at Leatherhead include the architect Lord Richard Rogers; band leader Victor Sylvester; Francis Rossi, front man of rock group Status Quo; Sir Anthony Hope, author of *The Prisoner of Zenda*; and Gavin Hewitt, the BBC reporter.

The London College of Divinity

After the departure of the St John's Foundation School, the two properties in Mortimer Road stood empty until the London College of Divinity took over St John's Hall in 1863. Rev. Alfred Peache and his sister Kezia Peache had inherited a substantial fortune from their father, a wealthy timber merchant and property owner. They were both devoted evangelists, determined to give their money to worthy causes. In 1863 they gave an initial sum of £35,000 to establish the London College of Divinity (also known as St John's Hall) in Kilburn. In all, they gave more than £100,000 to the college. The first principal was Thomas Pownall Boultbee (1818–1884) but he did not stay long, and in 1866 the College left Kilburn for Highbury, where it remained until 1940. Eventually the college moved to Nottingham, where it became part of the University.

Kilburn College

The building on the left in [26] had become a school again by the mid-1860s. 'Kilburn College' was run by Mr George Ogg, who steadily increased the standard and scale of education he offered, but it is not known whether his ability kept pace with his ambitions. In 1847 he was living in Brompton and running a small school providing 'education for six young gentlemen'. By 1856, Mr and Mrs Ogg had moved to Kilburn and occupied a pair of newly built houses, Nos.3 and 4 Mortimer Road. Here they opened 'Vere House', a 'Preparatory School for the Sons of Gentlemen'. The move to the larger house round the corner resulted in a change of direction and a new name: in 1864, prospective pupils at 'Kilburn College' were being offered a

'first-class education - classical, mathematical, and general and are prepared for Woolwich, Sandhurst and the public schools. The situation is elevated, the school rooms, dining room, lavatory, and dormitories lofty and spacious'.

Mrs Ogg's name had been removed from the prospectus and Mr Ogg now described himself as the school's Principal (University of London) and 'formerly instructor of HRH. the Prince of Wales'! George Ogg died in 1870 aged 60, but Kilburn College had closed the year before.

Mount Greville and the St Peter's Home

After Kilburn College left, the house reverted to a private residence. The eminent architect John Loughborough Pearson was commissioned to renovate the property for the new owner, **Benjamin Lancaster** (see p 98). He had made a fortune trading with his partner William Wilson in Russia, and by the manufacture of candles in England. Lancaster preferred the name 'Mount Greville' for the house rather than Greville Mount.

In 1851 Lancaster married Rosamira Bellairs and 10 years later the couple founded the Community of St Peter, a religious order devoted to nursing and providing convalescent care for patients discharged from hospital. They also trained young girls for domestic service. The Sisterhood's first house was at 27 Brompton Square, Kensington, where two Sisters cared for twelve convalescent patients. As the work grew, Lancaster bought (by 1870) the empty 'St Johns Hall' next to his own house and gave it to the St Peter's Sisterhood. This property was large enough to provide both a convalescent home and a base for the Order. After Lancaster left Kilburn in c.1880, the Sisterhood took over Mount Greville and the two houses were combined [27]. Pearson had previously built a chapel that linked the two houses, for joint use by the Lancasters and the Home. With glass and paintings by Clayton and Bell, it was described as 'one of the most beautiful private chapels in the country'. Lancaster also recommended Pearson to the building committee of St Augustine's Church, just across the Edgware Road, and he got the commission.

The founding of the St Peter's Sisterhood had caused controversy. It was said that some women who became novitiates had been prostitutes and the Home also took in their children, if they had any. Mrs Lancaster was condemned as 'facilitating vice'. Despite criticism, the Home flourished. The arrival of the Home in Mortimer Road clearly displeased Mr Brown in nearby North Hall. He complained to the authorities of covered corridors under construction against the boundary walls, that 'greatly obstructed' his view and 'seriously injured' his property. His complaint was judged to be groundless; indeed, as his house was separated from the Home by Harlestone Villa, it is hard to see how it could have been upheld.

A letter to *The Times* in 1892 from Canon Cooke said that since the Home had opened, the sisters had tended and consoled over 650 patients during their last days. These were described as poor ladies, wives and daughters of poor tradesmen, artisans, domestic servants and others.

In 1929, the Home advertised its services in the local Hampstead Directory. To modern eyes, they seem quite restrictive.

[27]
St Peter's Home, formerly Mount Greville (left) and St Johns Hall (right)]

The Home is for respectable sick persons who are members of the Church of England, of the following classes:
1. Women, either convalescent or acutely ill; in advanced phthisis or in the last stage of illness. Also those needing surgical or medical care but unsuitable for General Hospitals.
2. Children over two and under twelve years of age, of respectable parentage. Boys are only admitted under six years of age. No chronic invalids are received permanently. Patients suffering from cancer, mental diseases, fits, imbecility, ringworm or diseases caused by intemperance are ineligible.

Various weekly fees were charged; *'payments must be made a week in advance and are exclusive of wine and washing'*.

During WW II, the Home contacted Hampstead Borough Council in November 1941 asking that a shelter be constructed for staff and patients. The estimated cost of reinforcing the basement was £325, but while recognising the inmates were usually poor and the facility ran at a loss, the Council decided not to proceed, as it was unable to help a private institution. It was also possible that the Community would move out: only a small number of staff and six patients remained at the Home. The Assistant Mother Superior replied that they had every intention of remaining … 'unless it became impossible to do so', but in fact they had to: in 1944, the buildings were damaged by the V1 flying bomb that fell in the garden of North Hall and the Convent was evacuated to Woking. The buildings were demolished after the war and their sites now form part of the Mortimer Estate.

Benjamin Lancaster, candle manufacturer and philanthropist, c. 1806 to 1887

With his partner William Wilson, Lancaster founded (Edward) Price and Co, the candle-making firm. Lancaster had an aunt named 'Price', and they chose this name for their business rather than trade under their own. Tallow was one of Russia's major exports, and their expertise in this field probably led Wilson and Lancaster to buy a patent for processing coconut oil to make a solid fat substitute for tallow and oil for lamps. They opened a factory at Battersea, and by 1840 their candles, made from a blend of tallow and coconut oil, were flying off the production line. By 1901 the firm was the world's largest manufacturer of candles and is still trading today.

In 1841 and 1851, the census had Lancaster living at 40 Chester Terrace, Regent's Park. He married Rosamira Bellairs in June 1851 and 10 years later, the couple were at 1 Princess Terrace, shortly before moving to Kilburn. Rosamira died in 1874 and Lancaster had moved to Bournemouth by 1881. He died in Christchurch, Hampshire, in 1887 and left £135,000, with a bequest of £30,000 to the St Peter's Home. It seems probable Lancaster leased rather than bought the freehold of both the Mortimer Road houses, as by 1896 the Rates list their owner as 'Captain Bagot', who had inherited the Upton estate. Lancaster's funeral service was held at St Augustine's, Kilburn.

Susan Oldfield, the first Mother Superior of the Community, also died in 1887. The *Kilburn Times* reported that her funeral procession started from the Home in Mortimer Road, with over 200 Sisters in attendance. The service was held at St Augustine's and she was buried in Willesden Cemetery, Willesden Lane, where the Sisters owned a large plot.

The St Peter's Sisterhood has left an extensive archive, detailing the day-to-day running of the main Kilburn home and their other establishments (now at Surrey History Centre). The largest of the branch homes was at Woking. It opened as a Hospital for Incurables in 1885, paid for by Lancaster, in memory of his wife Rosamira. In 1892, the sisters accepted an invitation from Bishop Corfe to work among women in Korea, where they were involved in running an orphanage in Seoul and in nursing and evangelism. After the Sisters left Kilburn in 1944, Woking became the motherhouse, known as St Peter's Convent. In 1990, the Sisters moved into a smaller, purpose-built convent adjacent to the Woking building. This finally closed in 2004 because of a decline in numbers seeking to join the Order.

Henley House School, later Nos.1 and 2 Mortimer Place

Henley House, one of several private schools in the area, was housed in a pair of semi-detached houses in Mortimer Road, at the corner with Kilburn Priory. John Leeds was the owner and schoolmaster in 1871, when the census recorded his family plus nine pupil boarders and two assistant school masters as resident. Leeds was a member of the Greville Place Congregational Church and their records note he died suddenly of bronchitis on 23 April 1878.

The school was bought by John Vine Milne who paid £100 for the goodwill which consisted of

twenty or thirty desks and half-a-dozen inky boys whose parents had been too lazy to find a better school for them. Henley House was one of those private schools, then so common, now so unusual, for boys of all ages. (It) drew its boys from the region of Maida Vale and St Johns Wood; the parents were theatrical, artistic, professional and business people who from motives of economy or affection preferred to have their sons living at home.

Matters at Henley House improved slightly under Milne's management, although the school was never a financial success. But Milne's style of teaching was enlightened for the times. He did not believe in corporal punishment or threats, and would not tolerate bullying, believing school should be a happy place.

J V Milne's son was Alan Alexander Milne, better known as A A Milne, the author of *Winnie the Pooh*. Alan was born at Henley House four years after the family moved to Mortimer Road, and in his autobiography *It's too late now*, he recalled much about his childhood days in Kilburn, the school and the neighbourhood. The two houses in Mortimer Road were divided between school and family rooms, an arrangement common to many such establishments. The rear gardens were thrown into one and gravelled over to provide a playground, which included a scaffold structure called 'The Gymnasium'. Milne writes:

Henley House was two houses. On the Family Side you entered the front door and found yourself in a small lobby. Opening the coloured-glass door of the lobby, you came into the 'hall', a hall no bigger than was determined by the junction of a broad staircase with the passage. The first door on the left led into the drawing-room. The next door led into the sitting room, and through the door opposite we went into the big schoolroom which was the corresponding drawing-room and sitting-room thrown into one. To return to our own side of the house. At the end of the passage was the music-room, having a piano in it. We now open a door on the right and fall down some stairs into the basement. Beneath the drawing-room was the kitchen (and) beneath the sitting-room was what the rest of the school called The Kids' Room. Here we ate, lived, worked, played with our governess and when we were part of the school, was still our home from home.

In 1889, a young H G Wells joined the staff as its first science master. In his eyes, the school houses had been 'very roughly adapted' and he was scathing about the type of education provided by Henley House and by the many other schools of its type then existing. '*They were still responsible for the education, or want of education, of a considerable fraction of the British middle-class. They were under no public control at all. Anyone might own one, anyone might teach in one, no standard of attainment was required of them'.* Wells believed modern schools should provide their pupils with a social and political outlook on life.

But Wells was generous about J V Milne, 'a really able teacher' who cared about his pupils.

> *Milne was a man who won my unstinted admiration and remained my friend throughout life; nevertheless it is useless to pretend that Henley House was more than a sketch of good intentions ….We taught them a few tricks, we got them a few 'certificates,' we did something for their manners and their personal bearing, we dropped some fruitful hints into them, but we gave them no coherent and sustaining vision of life. In making these criticisms I am not blaming J.V. Milne. In view of his conditions and resources he did wonderfully. He could hardly pay his way; he could not pick and choose his assistants; economies and compromises cramped his style.*

Milne had given H G Wells just £1 to buy new apparatus. There was already an aquarium stocked with 'all the animal life which the Leg of Mutton pond at Hampstead could show', but Wells also found a cupboard full of broken flasks. These had been carefully arranged by his predecessor who had broken them all in the course of a single lesson, trying to produce oxygen by heating potassium permanganate; the glass was not strong enough to withstand irregular heating over a Bunsen burner. One of Wells' pupils told him it had been 'a very great lesson indeed!'. Wells determined to put his experiments on the blackboard in future, although he did suggest dissecting a rabbit. Milne gave his cautious approval, so long as it would not be 'indelicate' - one never knows what parents will find to object to'. Wells taught at Henley House for a year, walking to Kilburn from his lodgings in Fitzroy Road, by Primrose Hill.

Alfred Harmsworth, the future Lord Northcliffe of publishing fame, was a pupil at Henley House, and had left before H G Wells was hired. But Alfred was still remembered by the staff and Wells wrote: 'He made a very poor impression on his teachers, and became one of those unsatisfactory, rather heavy, good-tempered boys who in the usual course of things drift ineffectively through school to some second-rate employment'. Wells went on to express the opinion that

> *it was JV's ability that saved him from that. Somewhere about the age of twelve, Master Harmsworth became possessed of a jelly-graph for the reproduction of MS. in violet ink, and with this he set himself to produce a mock newspaper. JV… encouraged young Harmsworth… to persist with the Henley House Magazine even at the cost of his school work.*

The rest, as they say, is history. Alfred's younger brother St-John was at the school when H G Wells was teaching. Wells called him 'a sturdy and by no means brilliant youngster' but he too went on to become a successful businessman: 'A year or so before he died I met him at Cannes, a princely invalid, the proprietor of Perrier, preposterously wealthy'.

J V Milne sold the school in 1893. As Alan said: 'Papa .. had been uneasy about Kilburn for some years. The neighbourhood was going down'. This comment may owe more to Milne's awareness of the cramped and unsanitary terraces the other side of Kilburn Priory than a general decline in the neighbourhood. More significant perhaps was an unexpected legacy that allowed Milne to fulfil his desire and establish a preparatory school for boys under 14. The family left Kilburn for Westgate-on-Sea.

In 1895 Rev. George Forrester Watson occupied the two Mortimer Road houses and by 1901 the census shows that Henley House School was in the hands of Charles Vincent Godby, who had previously run a private school in Petersham in Surrey. The houses were later renumbered as 1 and 2 Mortimer Place and reverted to two separate houses for private tenants. They were both demolished as part of the Kilburn Gate scheme (p 27) and no photographs have survived, but it seems probable they looked very like the surviving villas in nearby Mortimer Crescent.

Alan Alexander Milne, author, 1882–1956

Alan's grandfather travelled to Jamaica as a missionary. He married there, and John Vine Milne was born before the couple returned to England. John married a fellow teacher, Maria Heginbotham. They had three sons, Barry, Kenneth and Alan, who was the youngest. In a photograph taken about 1886, the brothers have 'Little Lord Fauntleroy' lacy collars and curls – like 'Shirley Temple', Alan wrote later. As a boy growing up in Henley House, Alan explored the surrounding area with Ken and Barry, on foot and later venturing further afield on bicycles. The boys were allowed a great deal of freedom, running through the streets with their iron hoops as far as the Bayswater Road on one occasion. Alan recalled the open countryside near the school: fighting a boy in St Mary's Fields, as the area on either side of Priory Road was called before the houses were built; and hunting with the family dog in fields off the Finchley Road. Eventually the boys were sent away to school, and at the end of Alan's first term at Westminster, the Milnes left Henley House to start a new school in Thanet.

Alan went to Westminster School like his elder brother Kenneth, and then on to Cambridge. He started work as assistant editor of *Punch* in 1906 and served in WW I as a signals officer. Despite writing many adult books and plays, he is best remembered for his children's poetry and for creating Winnie the Pooh, which immortalised his son Christopher Robin as the young boy in the stories. Milne died in 1956.

Henry George (Harry) Batsford, publisher and author, 1880–1951

Batsford was educated at Henley House School, where his science master was H G Wells. In 1897 Harry entered the bookselling and publishing firm founded by his grandfather. He became chairman and managing director of B T Batsford Ltd in 1917 and remained so until his death. In the 1920s and 1930s he introduced fully illustrated books on architecture and the topology of Britain, which gave the term 'a Batsford book' a recognised significance. He wrote several of these himself under a pseudonym. He died in Paddington Hospital on 20 December 1951 from barbiturate poisoning which was self-administered. The coroner delivered an open verdict on the circumstances of his death.

Harlestone Villa, later No.6 Mortimer Place

Harlestone Villa was probably built for its first owner, Edward William Stanley, who took a 99-year lease on part of the aptly named 'Hilly Field' in 1853. Shown as a 'bank clerk' in the 1851 census, he was then living in Westbourne Park with his wife Amelia. They had moved into their new Kilburn home by September 1854. The details of a later sale given below show the house as a substantial one, so it seems likely Stanley had a supplementary source of income. In 1856, he was one of several local residents who contributed to the building fund for St Mary's Church in Abbey Road, for which he also acted as co-treasurer.

Stanley was married at least three times. Amelia died after a short illness on

Christmas Day, 1873. He next married widow Mrs Anna Chaplin Leveridge in 1875. The couple had no children and she died in 1878. Stanley's third wife was Fanny Rowe, nearly 30 years his junior, whom he married in 1880. She survived her husband and moved to Kensington after Stanley died in 1889. He was buried in Hampstead Cemetery, Fortune Green (where he was joined by Fanny in 1925). Stanley's gravestone gives his place of residence as Kilburn, but 2 years later when Harlestone Villa came up for sale, it was firmly advertised as being in St Johns Wood.

A charming long leasehold, detached Residence, with tastefully laid out and well shrubbed grounds. It contains on the first floor four bedrooms, dressing and bath rooms; on the ground floor, spacious entrance hall, conservatory leading into billiard room, a noble drawing-room with bay window, opening into a library; basement, housekeeper's room, kitchen, and well arranged domestic offices. Rental value of £130 per annum, lease unexpired of about 62 years.

The house did not sell immediately, but instead was rented. In 1891, the Scottish baritone **Andrew Black** moved in with his new wife, Zoe, and they called the house St Andres Villa. The couple left Kilburn (probably during Borglum's residence, see below) and in 1901 were living in 40 Bramham Gardens, Kensington, but they returned briefly to Mortimer Road in 1904 and 1905.

From 1899 to about 1902 the American sculptor and painter **John Gutzon Mothe Borglum** lived and worked from the house. Borglum left his studio in West Kensington for Kilburn. Here he painted murals for private homes, but he is best known for the giant heads of US presidents carved into the summit of Mount Rushmore. In 1901, the young daughter of a Californian friend came to stay at Harlestone Villa. Her name was Isadora Duncan and she danced for Borglum on the villa's large lawn, scattering rose petals behind her.

In 1905, **William Reynolds-Stephens** bought the remainder of the lease of Harlestone Villa from the third Mrs Stanley for £1,375, and almost immediately embarked on a major remodelling programme. Reynolds-Stephens was another artist and sculptor, one of many who appear to have been attracted to this neighbourhood by the size of the properties and the associated work space. He got permission to convert the billiard room and an adjoining room into a studio, creating a second studio behind this, linked to the drawing room by a glass corridor. Although the house was now almost doubled in size, it still possessed a huge garden.

Reynolds-Stephens lived at Harlestone Villa until he died in 1943, submitting over 60 pieces to the Royal Academy Show from this address, which became the more prosaic '6 Mortimer Place' after the road was renamed in 1915. He was a great collector and picked up many bargains at the Caledonian Market in London. His collection of Oriental costumes, head-dresses, mirrors and other antiques filled many rooms in the beautiful house at Mortimer Place, many features of which he had himself decorated. The house with its 'delightful old matured shady garden' and all its contents were auctioned in November 1943, when many Oriental items went under the hammer. It is not known whether the property sold, but in the following year the neighbouring house was badly damaged by a flying bomb, and Harlestone Villa was also probably affected. Its site now forms part of the Kilburn Gate estate.

Andrew Black, singer, 1859–1920

Black was a Scottish baritone, who studied in London and Italy. His London premiere was at the Crystal Palace in 1887, and he toured abroad as well as widely in the UK, enjoying great success in several operatic roles. Black was appointed professor of music when the Manchester Royal College of Music was established in 1893 but he finally settled in Australia, where he died in Sydney, on 15 September 1920. His occupation of 'St Andres' was broken by what was probably an 1899-1902 sublet to Borglum (see below), as Andrew Black is again briefly listed at the house during 1904-1905. Zoe de Bernay was a widow when she married Black in 1891.

John Gutzon Mothe Borglum, sculptor and artist, 1867–1841

Born in Idaho in 1871, Borglum was of Swedish extraction. He studied art in California and at the École des Beaux Arts in Paris. Commissions were thin on the ground when he moved to London in the 1890s. He wrote:

I have had the disturbing pleasure of being called 'master' by the French critics and some Americans, yet at the moment I cannot spend sixpence without wondering where the next one will come from.

Borglum returned to the USA in 1901, but immediately received a commission from England – for twelve painted panels to be installed in the Midland Railway Company's new hotel in Manchester. The fee was 5000 guineas, but the terms were cash on delivery. Borglum accepted the commission, returning to England in 1903 to supervise installation of the panels. They depicted scenes from *A Midsummer's Night's Dream* and the Court of King Arthur. Actually, Borglum was primarily a sculptor, specialising in enormous figures in stone and bronze. He is best known for the gigantic heads of the presidents at Mount Rushmore, South Dakota completed in 1939. A short documentary film was made about this project entitled *The story of Mt Rushmore: America in stone* (1994). Borglum died in Chicago in March 1941, aged 73.

Sir William Ernest Reynolds-Stephens, artist and sculptor, 1862–1943

Reynolds-Stephens moved to Kilburn from nearby Hill Road, St John's Wood. Born in Detroit to British parents, his father's name being Stephens: William added 'Reynolds' in 1890. He studied art at the Royal Academy Schools and painted mainly historical and legendary subjects, but after 1894 he devoted all his time to sculpture. Reynolds-Stephens experimented with materials, often combining several in a single work, and he believed there was no better place to display sculpture than in the open air. Tate Britain owns *The Royal Game* (1911), depicting Queen Elizabeth I and Philip II playing chess – an allegory of the battle between Spain and England. Knighted in 1931, Reynolds-Stephens made a number of memorials and sculptures in churches, as well as War Memorials for the Boer War and WW I.

It is evident from many of the artists' biographies that they knew and socialised with one another. Reynolds-Stephens' style was influenced by fellow sculptor Alfred Gilbert, who lived in Maida Vale from 1893 to 1901. As President of the Royal Society of British Sculptors, Reynolds-Stephens was instrumental in awarding their Gold Medal to Gilbert in 1926. When Gilbert died in 1934, Reynolds-Stephens was asked to make his death mask. Another close friend was Frank Salisbury, a talented portrait painter, who built a house on the corner of Platts Lane and West Heath Road, which he called 'Sarum Chase'. Sir William designed a fountain for the grounds of the house. Salisbury said of his friend *'his work will stand when all the words lightly spoken are forgotten in oblivion'*.

8   Kilburn High Road, Alexandra Road and other streets

KILBURN HIGH ROAD

The only original buildings that have survived (although rebuilt more than once) are The Red Lion and The Bell public houses.

Goubert's Kilburn Nursery

Jean-Baptiste Goubert's nursery and florists occupied a large triangular site at No.2 Kilburn High Road. The building and a number of glasshouses were situated at the junction of the main road and Kilburn Priory [28]. This was one of four local Goubert businesses; he also owned a nursery alongside Kilburn Underground Station and in Brondesbury Park as well as a florist's shop at 67 Kilburn High Road. Goubert was born in France and worked in the Kilburn business before taking it over in the 1870s. By 1881 he employed 32 workers. This photograph was taken after Goubert died in 1894, and the notice shows the premises as 'sold'. The nursery ground was cleared about 1899, but the Goubert family continued to trade from one of the new shops that were built on Kilburn High Road. The expansion of Goubert's business reflected the development of Kilburn, growing as new roads and houses were built and gardens were laid out.

[28] Goubert's nursery, sold after Jean-Baptiste's death in 1894 © M Colloms

Kilburn Empire Music Hall and Cinema

When Goubert's Nursery closed at the end of the 1890s a run of shops was built on the main road called 'The Parade' and part of the site was used for the Kilburn Empire. The first ornate building was built in 1906 to plans by the architect Hingston, who also designed other theatres. There were problems obtaining a full licence

and the noted theatre architect W G R Sprague was brought in to redesign the building. It opened in April 1908 as a music hall and circus, with traps and pits to house the animals included under the stage. Local resident George Dunn recalled the event:

Its inaugural week was given over to an entire performance by "the great Lafayette," mystery man and animal trainer.

Lafayette, whose real name was Sigmund Neuberger, was the highest paid artist of the time. But 3 years after appearing in Kilburn he met a tragic death when the Empire Theatre in Edinburgh burned down in May 1911. As 'the Great Lafayette' took his bow at the end of his act a lamp fell onto the scenery, which instantly caught fire. A mass of flame shot over the footlights to the stalls. The audience, accustomed to unusual effects, were slow to recognise the danger. Only when the fire curtain was lowered did they hurry to the exits. By this time the stage was an inferno. It took 3 hours to bring the fire under control, and eleven people died. As well as the Great Lafayette, they included members of the orchestra, stage hands, a midget in the act called Little Joe and Alice Dale, a tiny 15-year-old girl who operated a scene-stealing mechanical teddy-bear.

The Kilburn Empire seated nearly 2000 people; it later changed its name to the Kilburn Vaudeville Theatre and back to the (New) Kilburn Empire. As a music hall, great stars such as Marie Lloyd, George Robey and Houdini (in 1909), played there.

George Dunn remembered one particular performance in June 1922:

[29] Programme at the Kilburn Empire, March 1918 (© M Colloms)

For about a quarter of an hour the O'Gorman Brothers "gagged" in the most clever fashion owing to the non-appearance of the next artist. This was Marie Lloyd, who was too ill to appear, and the tragic part was that it was her last week's engagement there.

The stage paper *Encore* wrote that Marie was 'at the top of her form' during her Kilburn Empire performances, but in fact she was exhausted and suffering from over-work. She died suddenly the following October.

Shows ran twice nightly **[29]** throughout the year, and the ladies in the audience were 'Respectfully Requested To Remove their Hats To Afford a Better View to Persons Seated Behind' Some of the artists they saw were:

Natalia and Diana (lady aerial gymnasts) Baby Vi Davis, (wonderful juvenile mime) The Pasquale Boys (World Famous Equilibrists), Joe Archer (the Cheerful Chappie), Ruffells Imperial Bioscope, Rinaldo (the Wandering Violinist), Mooney and Holbein (the Vaudevillians), Flora Cromer (the Lavender Girl), and Jordan and Harvey (Murderers of the Queen's English.)

Although films were shown from the outset, in the 1920s live acts still took precedence, with films run only on Sundays. The building was renamed The Essoldo in 1949 after it had been converted to a modern cinema. The stage was used on Sunday to broadcast the popular BBC live radio show, 'Variety Bandbox'. It was renovated in 1970, when the Edwardian façade was covered with an ugly metal cladding and substantial changes were made to the auditorium, so that no trace of the original fittings was visible. In 1972 it became The Classic Cinema but this closed a year later. It reopened as The Broadway Theatre in 1973, offering live shows. In 1976 'The Cycle Sluts' topped the bill, and *The Times* reported:

'a troupe of bearded and moustached Americans who wear high piled wigs, five inch eyelashes, garish makeup and an assortment of black studded corsets, brassieres, stocking belts and fishnet tights. The Sluts ("we couldn't even get our name printed on the posters for Chicago, dear"), went out onto Kilburn High Road for photographs. An elderly woman walking past said she was not surprised to be confronted by a large bearded man with a hairy stomach wearing a brassiere with springs sprouting from it. "We see all sorts of things in Kilburn, you know", she said with equanimity.'

The venue later reverted to films, and finally closed its doors in 1981. It lay derelict until 1984, when a religious group took over for a while. Its final use was by Quazar Lazar as a paintball game centre. Plans were made to demolish it, along with all the buildings on the triangle of land bordered by the High Road, Greville Road and Kilburn Priory, to be replaced by a new 700-seat cinema plus shops, offices and a hotel. In 1993 local opposition forced the developers to give up the idea of a cinema and reduce the height of the development on the Kilburn Priory side as well as set back the building line here. Demolition followed a year later and the site was redeveloped as the Regents Plaza Hotel, opened 1996; it is currently the London Marriott Hotel, Maida Vale. In 2006 a new library opened on the corner with Greville Road.

Oliver Goldsmith, writer, poet

The writer Oliver Goldsmith is believed to have lived in a cottage on the east side of the Edgware Road near Kilburn Priory, where he wrote *The history of Earth and Animated Nature*. This was published in 1774, the year Goldsmith died. The journal *Mirror of Literature, Amusement, and Instruction* for 10 March 1832 reported that Goldsmith's wooden cottage was still standing, although the surrounding area had been covered with newly erected villas. Five years later *The Times* of 16 September 1837 reported that 'the cottage was pulled down last Thursday to make way for improvements to the area'. After much research we now believe that the cottage stood on the main road next to 'St Mildred's Cottage' and they formed a pair of houses. Baines (1890) provides a description of them:

> Both were painted white and each had a door in the centre, protected by a porch and flanked by a veranda, and each possessed two windows on the ground floor and three above.

Goldsmith's cottage was demolished when Belsize Road was widened, possibly in association with railway building, so it would have been under the current Belsize Road. St Mildred's was pulled down later and a Bank was built in 1875 on the corner of Belsize Road; this is currently occupied by Holland and Barrett, the health food shop.

SPRINGFIELD LANE

All but four of the original properties, now Nos.6-12 even, have been demolished.

Nos.27 and 29 Springfield Lane, previously Nos.7 and 8 Springfield Villas, Goldsmith's Place

By 1879, Miss Emma Newbery had established a Home for Blind Children at 107 Portsdown Road, Maida Vale, where she was living in 1883. She also opened a School and Home for Blind Children in the semi-detached 7 and 8 Springfield Villas, offering training to the pupils. The 1881 census shows a school with 32 blind pupils here; it may have replaced the Portsdown Road establishment which had closed by then. The school was still operating in 1896 but shut soon afterwards.

By 1901, the houses were owned by the large drapers store William Roper and Co. (p 22) on Kilburn High Road, and were used as staff accommodation. The houses were demolished during the 1950s redevelopment of this area; their sites now form part of the 'Goldspring Estate'.

ALEXANDRA ROAD, now LANGTRY ROAD (see map on p 83)

On the Upton estate:

North side: Originally, 192a, 192-166 even Alexandra Road. All demolished, except for 1-9 odd Langtry Road, previously 192a, 192-186 even Alexandra Road. By the late 1890s an extension was built in the gardens of No. 192. By 1904 this had become a self-contained dwelling, numbered 192a.

South side: 143-141 odd (demolished)

Alexandra Road, the last road to be completed on this part of the Upton estate and situated between the railway and Mortimer Road, was laid down soon after 1863-4. It ran from Kilburn Priory onto the neighbouring Eyre property and continued on the other side of Abbey Road. This book covers only the properties on the Upton estate.

Post-WWII clearance and redevelopment has resulted in the demolition of all but five properties: Nos.192a, 192–186, renumbered as 1-9 odd, Langtry Road. The remainder of the houses on the northern frontage have been replaced by the Langtry Children's Centre, which opened in July 1974. The road was originally named in honour of Alexandra, the Princess of Wales; the irony of renaming the road after one of her husband's mistresses was clearly lost on Camden Council. Lillie Langtry, known as the 'Jersey Lily', lived in Leighton House, Alexandra Road on the other side of Abbey Road during the 1870s.

No.166 Alexandra Road

Samuel Joseph Dainton, local tradesman and councillor, d. 1910

Dainton was one of the many builders who helped create Victorian Kilburn. Originally from Somerset, when he and his family were living over their shop in Belsize Road in 1881, the business already employed 50 men and boys. He had moved to Alexandra Road by 1901. Dainton served as a Kilburn Ward councillor for 17 years and was described as an 'old and much respected resident of the Borough' when he died in 1910. Then living at 154 Alexandra Road, Dainton was buried in the family grave at Hampstead Cemetery, Fortune Green Road.

Over the years, the census shows several of the houses in Alexandra Road inhabited by artists, some of whom appear to have made little headway in their chosen field while others achieved greater fame.

No.170 Alexandra Road

George Koberwein, artist, 1820–1876

In 1861, the Koberwein family were living in St John's Wood. The two daughters Rosa and Georgina were, like their parents, born in Austria. By 1871 they had moved to Alexandra Road. George Koberwein was (inaccurately) described the year before he died as 'a Russian artist of repute'. In fact he had lived in Vienna before settling in England. He specialised in portraits, in crayon and oils, and painted several members of the Royal Family. By 1876 the family were living at 182 Holland Road. Both his daughters became artists. Georgina produced still-life paintings and later portraits, exhibiting at the Royal Academy from 1876 to 1878. She exhibited under her married name of Mrs Terrell from 1879 to 1903.

No.172 Alexandra Road

Harry Leslie, artist

During the 1870s, Harry Leslie received some good reviews for his landscape paintings. He exhibited two paintings at the Royal Academy from this address, in 1877 and again in 1878.

No.176 Alexandra Road

Edwin Wensley Russell, painter, d. 1878

Russell painted portraits, genre and historical subjects. He lived at 10 Alexandra Road when he exhibited at the RA from 1869 to 1871. He is shown at 176 Alexandra Road only in 1873. He had moved to Alma Square by 1875 and died there in 1878.

No.3 Langtry Road, previously No.192 Alexandra Road

Edward Charles Barnes, artist

The 1881 census shows Edward Charles Barnes living here with his family. He describes himself as 'an artist, figure'. Daughter Emily, aged 18, was also an artist. Barnes was born in Birmingham, and painted genre, contemporary and domestic scenes, some with a Spanish theme. He exhibited at the RA between 1856 and 1882.

Charles Napier Kennedy, artist, 1852–1898

Moving to Kilburn from St George's Square, Pimlico, Kennedy submitted six paintings to the Royal Academy from Alexandra Road, between 1883 and 1885. He first specialised in portraits and later worked on mythological scenes. He probably moved in after Barnes left, but by 1886 Kennedy was living at 38 Avenue Road. He died in St Ives in 1898. His works are in many provincial galleries including Leeds, Sheffield, Liverpool and Manchester. His wife Lucy Marwood was also a painter.

Isaac Snowman, artist, 1873–1947

The *Jewish Chronicle* reported Isaac Snowman's death with the following words: '*a link with the artistic life of Hampstead at the turn of the century has been severed*'. Born in London, the son of a picture dealer, the 1881 census shows 7-year-old Isaac living with his parents at 297 Euston Road. Isaac moved to Kilburn during the 1890s, to a house in Oxford Road on the other side of the High Road and rented a studio at 192 Alexandra Road, from 1896 to 1898. He was a friend of Israel Zangwill, a founder member of 'The Wanderers of Kilburn', who also lived in Oxford Road (see also Arthur Davis, p 76). Snowman attended the Royal Academy Schools and studied in Paris under Bouguereau and Constant. He exhibited 18 works at the Royal Academy between 1893 and 1904: titles included *Tales of a Grandfather* and *The Wailing Wall, Jerusalem*. The latter was painted after a visit to Jerusalem with Zangwill. Snowman became a fine portrait painter and was commissioned to paint portraits of King George V and King Edward VII. He left Alexandra Road for various addresses in West Hampstead and Brondesbury; No.192 had become yet another school by 1899.

Snowman married Pearl Alexander in 1898, but in 1909 Pearl petitioned for divorce, on grounds of Isaac's desertion and adultery. The couple had lived together in Hampstead and Algiers, but Pearl claimed the marriage had been unhappy, '*owing to her husband's exaggerated views on the subject of "wifely obedience"*'. In August 1907 Snowman had gone to Africa to fulfil a commission for the King of Dahomey. A year later, in July 1908, Pearl wrote to Isaac asking him to come home, but he failed to do so. She asked for a divorce when she learned that Isaac had stayed with a woman in a London hotel during September 1908, signing the register as 'Mr and Mrs Snowman'. There were a few difficult moments when witnesses failed to recognise Snowman because he had grown a beard in Africa, but the handwriting in the register was positively identified as his, and Pearl got her divorce.

Snowman later commissioned the first house to be built in Ranulf Road off Finchley Road, which included work space: completed in about 1911, for many years it was simply known as 'The Studio'. Snowman emigrated to Palestine, where he set up a studio in Jerusalem. In 1921 he suffered a knife wound in the neck during a period of unrest. He later returned to England, where he died in 1947. His brother Emanuel was twice Mayor of Hampstead.

No.1 Langtry Road, previously No.192a Alexandra Road

Currently this is a separate house, but originally it was a studio attached to the main house next door. Isaac's younger brother **Louis Snowman**, also an artist, lived here from about 1904 to 1960.

Main sources

Aston, Mark (1997). *The Cinemas of Camden.* Camden Local History Archives, London

Baines, F E, ed. (1890). *Records of the manor, parish, and borough of Hampstead.* Whittaker and Co., London

Dye, Ira (1994). *The fatal cruise* (book on Captain John Maple). US Naval Institute, Annapolis, Maryland.

Electoral Rolls for Hampstead and St Marylebone.

Graves, Algernon (1973). *Dictionary of artists who exhibited in the principal London exhibitions 1760 to 1893.* Kingsmead Reprints, Bath (originally published 1895).

Graves, Algernon (1906). *Royal Academy of Arts: exhibitors 1769-1904.* George Bell and Sons, London.

Hampstead Borough Council Minutes

Hampstead and Highgate Express

Hampstead Vestry Minutes

Holder, M. and Gee, C. (1980) *The diary of a London schoolboy.* Camden History Society, London.

Hughes, Richard (2005). *Those things which are above: the history of St John's School, Leatherhead.* Gresham Books, Leatherhead.

Irvine, L. and Atterbury, P. (1998). *Gilbert Bayes, sculptor.* Richard Dennis Publishers, Shepton Beauchamp.

London County Council. *Names of streets and places in the administrative county of London.* 3rd Edition, 1929 and 4th Edition, 1955.

London Metropolitan Archives

London Street Directories

Master, B. (2001). *The Dukes.* Pimlico Publishers, London.

Milne, A A.(1939). *It's too late now.* Methuen, London.

Oppenheimer, Sir Francis (1960). *Stranger within.* Faber and Faber, London.

Pocock, T. (1996) *Travels of a London schoolboy.* Historical Publications, London.

Rate books of Hampstead and St Marylebone.

RIBA archive

Royal Academy of Arts: exhibitors 1905-1970. (1981) E.P. Publishing, Wakefield.

Royal Academy of Arts: exhibitors 1971-1989. (1989) Hilmarton Manor Press, Calne.

Soden, J. (1996), *The Society of Woman Artists: exhibitors 1855-1996.* Hilmarton Manor Press, Calne.

The Builder

The Jewish Chronicle

The Kilburn Times

Thompson, F M L. (1974). *Hampstead, building a borough, 1650-1964.* Routledge Kegan Paul, London.

Thwaite, A. (1990). *A. A. Milne, his life.* Faber and Faber, London.

Weindling, G. and Colloms, M. (1999). *Kilburn and West Hampstead Past.* Historical Publications, London.

Wells, H G. (1966). *Experiment in autobiography, vol.1.* Gollancz, London (originally published in 1934).

Who's Who? and *Who Was Who?*

Online sources

Ancestry: Census data from 1841 to 1901

Ancestry: London telephone directories

Google searches of the Internet

Groves' New Dictionary of Music and Musicians

National index of births, marriages and deaths

Oxford Dictionary of National Biography

The Times Digital Index

Wills on line

Index